The Properties

Also by Colin Browne

Abraham
Ground Water*
The Shovel*

*Available from Talonbooks

The Properties

Colin Browne

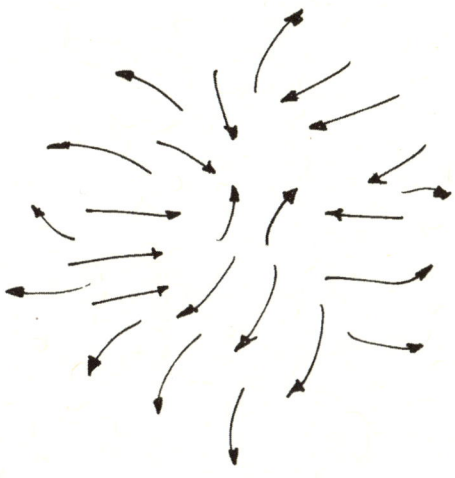

TALONBOOKS

Talonbooks
P.O. Box 2076, Vancouver, British Columbia, Canada V6B 3S3
www.talonbooks.com

Typeset in Sabon.
Printed and bound in Canada on 50% post-consumer recycled paper.
Typeset & cover design by Overleaf.

First printing: 2012

The publisher gratefully acknowledges the financial support of the Canada Council for the Arts, the Government of Canada through the Canada Book Fund and the Province of British Columbia through the British Columbia Arts Council and the Book Publishing Tax Credit for our publishing activities.

Grateful thanks are due to the editors of the journals where some of these poems have previously appeared in an earlier version: *The Capilano Review* and *subTerrain*. An earlier version of "A Capillary Manifesto" was published as a broadsheet by the SFU Gallery and exhibited in the SFU Tech Gallery in Vancouver, British Columbia.

Library and Archives Canada Cataloguing in Publication

Browne, Colin, 1946–
      The properties / Colin Browne.

Poems.
Includes bibliographical references.
ISBN 978-0-88922-685-2

      I. Title.

PS8553.R69P76 2012   C811'.54   C2011-908719-7

for
my family
near and far

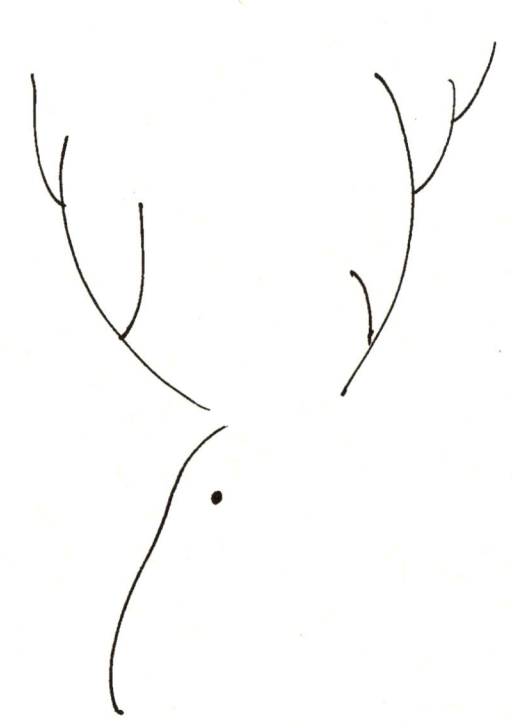

But Nature, that knows best its own laws, and the several properties of bodies, knows also best how to adapt and fit them to her designed ends, and whoso would know those properties, must endeavour to trace Nature in its working, and to see what course she observes.

ROBERT HOOKE, *"Observ. XXXV. Of the contexture and shape of the particles of* Feathers," *Micrographia: or some Physiological Descriptions of Minute Bodies made by Magnifying Glasses with Observations and Inquiries thereupon*

fish *and* fowl

that's it

that's us

O

my
          crimson

pronoun, my
my, my

plotter

my tear
my mouth

knew its
name before

I did

imperium

(when they
were small

they laughed
and giggled

and rolled
around like

puppies)—and
then wham!

it hits
me, how

"The West,"
our roaring

phantom, is
an antlered

man and
his song

is an
elegy

prickle operas

floss boats
fleet groats
fish flits
flip slits
stale oafs
fig stoles
neat floes
nose fleet
flea's stone
so toned
fish sit
snot floats
flat stoats
flip sheets
fillet milt
stone boats
false notes
flip out
flense a lot
furtive eels
noah's fleet
scan atone
slit fish
stone flab
fickle stem
stoat phlegm
teen scud
mean falsies
storm slab
five gloats
fore motes

stow moans
fluke sheet
my sleet
flea glee
fire's out
fort doubt
ice faux
foe's pant
flesh mash
fog fight
quick dick
plinth rinse
frog glub
armed legs
smolt punt
peeled glands
atom oil
fond scabs
scant fronds
false teens
spot rue
jam cog
goat's oak
asp puke
skim freak
swine pumps
wise gobs
five skins
moat eels
flag spots
dime bogs

rat domes
scone dogs
rose wart
bright eyes
olm nose
goose bang
cud bling
long cod
old stick
skin fork
wet cuke
red knee
reed boar
red bum
red lips
my sweet

A Perfect Stranger

Crushed Blacks; or, A Blown White Is a Big Three
For Victor Browne (1918–1994)

O l'Oméga, rayon violet de Ses Yeux!
ARTHUR RIMBAUD, "Voyelles"

Next in order we shall have to legislate about the horse contests.
PLATO, *Laws* VIII

A sack of
vowels

dropped
into a mouth

of ice.
The fugue

that sang him awake
at night.

He had the horse right there.
He was the snow

I shovelled before school.
When he lay beside

my mother in the dark, who wrote
those jokes?

Those hands knew
infant joy.

It was consonants
I wanted

gnawing *&* messy
in the walls.

> *Down by the salley gardens*
> *My love and I did meet;*
> *She passed the salley gardens*
> *With little snow-white feet.*

For my wallet I took
a snip of hair

and his bifocals. Lying in the darkness
with his mother—

who was *she* before madness?
Protestants, you got

your stick of gelignite.
So, so long, *grubby gods*.

Rosy finches in the quince,
marsh wrens' nests,

a whole-tone
fugue.

From a fishboat on the flood
in Booth Bay,

a stranger
to all
but himself.

My *Orphée*.

48°52'001"N
123°33'297"W

> *She bid me take life easy,*
>   *as the grass grows on the weirs;*
> *But I was young and foolish,*
>   *and now am full of tears.*

Every Noodle in the Soup

a word
for every
noodle in the
soup

a cockerel's
neck
too much like
a man's

a basilica
of sticks
on the outskirts
of somewhere

machetes
Lee-Enfields
our rusted
Blue Bird

who of us
was glowing
with
a secret?

do not
offend
against
birds

a daughter
from Trois-
Pistoles
by the grace

of God her
foot tapping
mother
while on

an island
of legislated
poverty
a child's

grace
reassembled
slivers of the
holy world

if we're
bound together
by prayer
what's

beached me
has left me
high
and dry

i saw Casper
he was
not
friendly

how do my
antlers grow?
the officers
at the academy

abolished
the allegory
then robbed
the cave

another's misery
is your
good fortune
they insist

Sout

A
straw
in

the
eaves
I

wear
on
my

sleeve
first
straw

in
a
bowl

of
straws

Love's Strange Vestibule

I'm drunk
on you
in this overpriced
steak house.
Couple more beers,
then I'll
take up your
crutches,
and make up
your bed,
old comrade.

You'll close
your eyes
on my sofa,
I'll turn down the TV.
How many years
has it been?
Opening our buckets
in the lunchroom,
peeling our eggs,
pitching apple cores
into the can?

We sold heavy equipment
north of North Bay,
and it's last call
in the old city,
we're talking year-end
and your philosophy
degree

and no, it's not
what you think,
not at all.

I gotta take a leak.
Let's go for a smoke
on the steps.

Here's the song
the orange
came from.

Two ryes.
Yes, that's it.

Love's getting stranger.
You're in danger
of finding out what
you're longing for.

What I Want to Say
For Peter Quartermain

The children seem to be fighting, but they are merely learning
to inhabit their country.
ROLAND BARTHES, "What Is Sport?"

What's that sound beneath our feet? Just seeds. In Saint-Jean we didn't need no love. We
had time, perched on counters in our gonch, spit-polishing boots. Chains, you say, that

you sang in like the what? We didn't see none. We smoked menthols. Had shower
parades in jockstraps, screaming. A plinth pierced a Sabre jet outside the Legion. We'd

mothers. They kept us like animals in their houses; later were we grateful. Anissimoff's
snuck into his room on Mondays and took his washing home. We were like dogs

hurtling alongside one another; if one got distracted or drowned the rest kept rushing on,
all snouts and pee. Should one stick a paw in a trap, well, chew off that leg and catch

up, three-legged dog! Skunk cabbage is a solid flame. We're less numerous now, and
love's hide is not like an Appaloosa's. Why'd she say *just* tulips? Alliteration. Tristan

rolled into the prompter's box. Plunge into his wake! I wrote, "*Our skins are not our own,*"
but crossed it out. That is, I think often of you with affection, my friend. That's what I

want to say. Leaves that green in the dusk. Is there a prototype? Marcello, or Rodolfo?
Forks flare, loop back and meet in a heart. We're just noisy cockerels, outshouting the

"uninterrupted disturbance of all social conditions, everlasting uncertainty *&* agitation"
(Marx). I close my eyes and see the little guy in his cap looking up to be adored. Bless

you, Peter; I open my eyes and friendship looks back. What's the ratio of *madness* to *gladness*? Is he an apocalyptic fellow, then? Not by nature. His ear? Think of a flicker's,

tuned to inner cadences. His dexterity in the northern dialects? Enduring. Is he kind? Infinitely. True? As a beam. For how long? To the end. My friend? I'll always wish it.

The Spirit

*Paalen's secret lies in having succeeded in seeing, in letting us see from the
inside of the bubble. That window overlooked a place bristling with totem
poles, not far from the city with a magical name: Vancouver, guarded by
the drumming of beavers on the water.*
ANDRÉ BRETON, "Wolfgang Paalen"

1

It might be a tool cart railing at a shop steward but it's the lilac
shift in weather, the alluvial, protracted pleats
of thunder, the sort of Manet sky a herring gull looks good against.
Abdomens of crane flies on the blue floor cast lean shadows,
the cat's thin, the past is pressing fiercely into
the vacuum of the now like air into a whoopee cushion.
That rash is as itchy as ever. Hordes of us think we know
what's right, or true, or something; why is that so akin to exile?
A plank floats into a cove, a *t* breaches a verb, horns blare.
What was it Stravinsky said? I'll look it up again. As far as I can tell,
everything's about to explode, overwhelmed by the interference of multiplying
analogical screens. Would you please try not to persuade me of anything,
just for a few numbers?

2

The hour of encounter, with creatures chewing, birthing,
caressing, filleting, fleecing, biting one another
to death. The painter showing up on a steamship
seventy years ago, at a shaman's grave. Another
scavenger of paradise. What then?
Writing to Breton, "the scenery resembles my paintings
more and more; here are the vast forests of my dreams ..."

A little like this young heron flying by
with his old man giving him hell, ducking under
a kingfisher, and what was it the ex-wife said yesterday,
laughing—she was in labour, she said—and she'd asked the ex-husband,
"What's the bird that flies like a fish swims?"

What did he make of his encounter with *this* invisible world,
or was it the father's fist?
It is always a fist.

3
Hinged to the unseen world a squall called Thebes
veers past the stone incisors, and tangled
in the pestled fantasies of his leashmen,
horns twitching, *paradisos* quivering, the painter in his Mackintosh
takes snapshots of a bear mother's
open womb and a stuffed whale's pizzle.
Far from Varengeville, entranced by "gleaming strangeness,"
by "an incomparable piece of fairy-tale."
Fairy tale my eye.

4
A daughter of the fold, known to us as *La Poitrine*,
asked me at the new moon
why I composed my own poems. "An active man of
your sensibilities, of your parts," said she,
taking the bull by the horns,

"a man who knows a stick from a stump, a thylacine
from a wolverine, should never find himself in the compromised position of
scribbling hurried stanzas to the crack of an invisible whip!
There are people who'll do that sort of thing for you."

5
What would you fetch at auction? Returns in Paris, at any rate, have been
disappointing. It may be time to pull in the horns. Some eras are not expansive.
Consider your original sensation on turning to the sketches of women
dancing through cracks with clackers in Bernard Bruyère's *Fouilles de Deir el-Médineh*.
Don't you want to dance with clackers too? Didn't they melt your bones?
You're probably recalling Stravinsky in London, November 1934, while
conducting the BBC Orchestra and dining, improbably, or perhaps not,
with Victor Gollancz. On two occasions the composer took Scottish smoked salmon
for hors d'oeuvres and the main course. Do you not see what I mean?
Reflect now on Bruyère's meticulous fifteen-volume reconstruction of Deir el-Medina,
the king suckled by a sycamore, and the artist's
village adjacent to the necropolis, seventy homes, seventy graves
for the makers of the king's tomb.
Now do you see what I mean?
Auden's creed was "work, carnival, and prayer," as he reminded Stravinsky.

6
You can't haul out "East St. Louis Toodle-Oo" without thinking,
"This is a five-act opera!"
No one can.

7

One discovers in almost every index consulted no reference at all to "Canada,"
a nation with reversing falls. This big, compromised lunkhead of a country
takes pride in its fecklessness. If Lauren Bacall came out for Canada,
I'd change my tune. I like older women. The citizens seem
cordial but proudly untutored, easily fitted with nose rings.
Their sons and daughters are airlifted off to war without
a whisper, it being peevish to raise a fuss.

A set piece in *Towards the Goal*, Mrs. Humphry Ward's effort to soften up
the Yanks in WWI, paints a picture, as they say, reminiscent of the simple,
spunky doughnut folk of the North, the hewers and fetchers who suffer silently
and whose eyes light up gratefully at portraits of their queen.
Mrs. Ward visits a "village mother" chivvied into cookery lessons by "ladies"
from the "food economy movement." She's on the verge of tears,
as my mother might have said, feeling helpless about her Arthur in France.
Mrs. Ward, in a passage of unadulterated shite, has her perk up:

> *Gloom descends on the little kitchen. The visitor is at a loss—*
> *when suddenly the round, motherly face changes.—"But there*
> *now! I'm goin' to smile, whatever 'appens. I'm not one as is*
> *goin' to give in! And we 'ad a letter from Arthur this morning,*
> *to say 'is company's on the list for leave, and 'e's applied.—*
> *Oh dear, Miss, just to think of it!"*

> *Then with a catch in her voice:*

> *"But it's not the comin' home, Miss—it's the goin' back again!*
> *Yes, I'll come to the cookin', Miss, if I possibly can!"*

> *There's the spirit of our country folk—patriotic, patient, true.*

Mrs. Ward, if you'll recall, opposed women's suffrage. If you had to choose,
would it be a loon's wail or Bubber Miley's *waa-waa* mute?
Miley and Duke are also absent from the indices.
In 1917, while *Towards the Goal* was being loaded into a transatlantic steamer,
Stravinsky and Picasso were arrested in Naples for peeing in the street.
That gorgeous, reckless horn is the magnificent sound of a cat pissing on Picasso's sun.
I've a mind to dance recklessly and play the clackers, to slip
my pelt on for the Lion Mother, Mistress of the Jingling Necklaces.

> *She is the lady of the dance wreaths,*
> *our lady of intoxication,*
> *we dance to none, we exalt none*
> *but her spirit.*

More attention might be paid to burials, crypts, necropoleis. They focus thought.
And to dancing.

Open and closed, open and closed—that's the sound of time.

Stag Beetle

I thought you were mine, but
you were sleeping.

In the Lane

Ye who hold your lives in hand—
Skimmers, who on oceans four
Petrels were, and larks ashore.
          HERMAN MELVILLE, "John Marr"

green quill
          seed pod
                    laburnum

under bitumen
          drill skyward
                    through asphalt,

magnolias
          from the smoking porch,
                    white cups, sparrows'

lips flushed with kissing
          finite *isn't*
                    is it not?

the fire in you
          that kindled me
                    ventre des vents

be fearless, pilgrim
          dare cosmologies
                    a mortal's more fun

than a god
      we didn't get to
           the *daube de lapin*

alas
      it's thirty years on
           but look, *petrel*

look, *lark*
      the holly's blooming,
           thrushes in the lane

will be lushes
      in the rain
           next winter

for Robin Blaser

The Last Word

Sir,

The Properties
For Tom Cone

*It seemed to me that I was looking at the form and pattern of a thought,
placed for the first time in finite space. Here space itself truly spoke,
dreamed, and gave birth to temporal forms ...*
> PAUL VALÉRY, reacting to Mallarmé's *Un coup de dés jamais
> n'abolira le hasard* in its intended manifestation, 1914

*You are going to exchange the misery of obstruction for the buoyancy
of construction.*
> LORD SOUTHBOROUGH to A. J. T. Taylor, June 17, 1936

In a cloud bones of steel.
> CHARLES REZNIKOFF, "The Bridge" in *Autobiography: New York*

*We have no vote. If we had it might be different, but as it is we are at the
mercy of those who have the vote and alas! They have no mercy.*
> CHIEF JOE CAPILANO, *Vancouver Daily World*, July 4, 1906

All the waters in the world collide in these narrows. The flood of what roars in and out grips and gives way, tearing us away from our self's edge like lassoed stars, tumbled in the tidal slap and lifted into the air, shedding scales, bones, shells, wings, nests cached in

the hearts of trees. Here there is only now, beyond *knowing*. These words are like a tea set in the corner of a dark room where the drapes have yet to be pulled aside. I stand in the shadow of the bridge; tires slam against the expansion plates in three-eight time.

Chain links rattle the wind. Where the table was set, the sand is sick. No one may enter. No one eats here now. Across the narrows, east of the fracture columns, wooden houses ran along the beach beneath the night sky, near those picnic tables. "That was my

grandmother's place," says my friend. A kingfisher lifts its head. Vancouver in May 1938, as the cable was being strung, would be familiar. The towers on Georgia Street that mime San José, Costa Rica, in 1971, are props. Pry them off their parking spirals and

you'll find the town as Captain David Bolster saw it: vain, thin skinned and on the make. You'd think scenery might elevate the soul. David was a little like a crocus. Salient, he knew, Red Cap, and *capriccio*, spoke wrench, gel. Every man may be a mark, but few are

as greedy as they are bewildered. Is destiny the prerogative of bossy stars, transmitted by invisible rays, or is life a fluke? What numbs a man into shame and resignation? A roofless hotel stands in the city's heart, with girders and rivet heads rusting in the rain.

The intersection's a sarcophagus to a ridge where seeds and spores nest like forest lint. A woman lugs home animals' hearts wrapped in brown paper. Gulls track the ferries across the harbour to a North Shore poxed with bulldozed clear-cuts. The burn piles

send up funnels of smoke. In 1931, speculators projected onto this slope the paranoia of their tribe, and pitched a pedicured enclave for their class and kind: white-fleshed and Christian (servants excepted)—an incubator for race renewal. The British Properties.

The mountainside could be had, unions were smarting and pliable; the *Übermenschen* pickled their property values in covenants. Even today hedges in the Properties do not exceed six feet, local trees twenty-five. No foreign trees are tolerated. None of this was

known to David Bolster, delivered, prematurely, in East London, four weeks before Zola's *J'accuse!* Am I mistaken to recall that these words were once recited in Canadian schools: "*Mon devoir est de parler; je ne veux pas être complice*"? The North Sea swallowed

his parents the night the *Condor* broke up off Cape Flattery. David and his sister, whom he'd never see again, were lodged with kin, in his case a disapproving aunt and her consumptive husband in Leeds. He took up piano and the bicycle, and with a precocious

affinity for Brahms became at twelve a regional prodigy. Astride The Kingfisher, a gleaming galaxy of tubes and spokes, he won the North of England Cup about the time de Chirico completed *Le cerveau de l'enfant* and was training for Le Tour of 1915. He

detrained in Amiens the following winter, a lieutenant in the 18th Cyclist Battalion. Preparing for the spring assault, Bolster and his "Mercuries" became masters of the Chinese attack. He and his tinkerers would slither toward the enemy in the morning

watch, hauling spools of wire and lifelike millboard dummies. In no man's land they'd rig their fatal theatre, hooking the decoy Tommies to high wires, then huddle in craters, clips at their cuffs. David once clung to the hand of a buried man in a blizzard,

reassuring him all night that help was on its way, before discovering there was no man. Come dawn they'd heave on the tripwires, the silhouettes sprang from their tombs; the Hun fired off a fusillade and the British artillery calibrated its guns. That was the idea.

There were long hours of discomfort and intimacy. Crouched in a metre of putrid water, threading pulleys through razor wire, what a rosy-cheeked captain and a hollow-eyed corporal might say to the other, or feel for the other, was their own damn beeswax.

Recovering in Hove from the jitters, David discovered the dummy factory nearby, and after lunch one day hitched a ride to propose the rewiring of a modified explosive trigger. He collided with Jean Moore, who did lips and eyebrows, in the hospital rose

garden, shaving armless men on her day off. He asked her to tea, talked about gearboxes and played scherzos. He drew stick unicyclists whistling down steeples. When it grew dark they were told go home. She'd ministered to intimate places and pieces of

men; this David was a beam of sunlight. "The way of a man with a maid," she thought. Jean broke off with her sapper. "'I'm sorry I am so thin and shaky,' said the Girl. 'I will be steady and plump soon, won't I?'" They fled on the day of demobilization. In Canada there

were posters: "No Brits Need Apply." Returned men thronged the streets. Jean got on as a night nurse in Toronto, David swept up at the track. Within a fortnight he was at Queen and Dufferin signing up for the Warrior's Day Parade, as unlikely an occurrence

at home as he could imagine. In the van, a nursing sister with a Croix de Guerre struggled to keep a delirious old man upright in a topless saloon, waving his arm as if it were a stick. Was that a VC on his tunic? A battalion of amputees came after, with the

. severely maimed in touring cars, then the blind and disabled from hospitals, clutching the fingers of sisters and decorated matrons, the Veterans of 1866, and then, as a mob, swarming the sidewalks and streetcar tracks, dark-faced men in medals, flushed, furious,

sweating. A piper from a Highland regiment tapped his deep reserves of humiliation. David Bolster found himself at the lake, the metal flange biting into his skin. A man fell to the street in convulsions. Gone their loopy grins. If the best had fallen, who were

they? Pursued by shame, waking up screaming in their boyhood beds, many had come to accept the imputations of moral deficiency. In the darkness with his porridge, David parsed the tactful obituaries. The world was a cesspit, much as he needed to pretend otherwise. Behind the smiles, truncheons. Behind the truncheons, the firing squad. And everywhere, hunger, influenza, the transparent uselessness of everything; children coughing up blood, women and men screwing in their filthy clothes, drunks shouting as

if they'd discovered a continent. Then the marching, fists in the street, police locking up ringleaders; mostly, according to the papers, foreign radicals. He thought too often of his landlady's daughter. He passed himself in the plate glass wearing the suit he'd worn

to his wedding. About this time, André Breton began to correct page proofs for Marcel Proust. The garden was overrun by rats in an ice storm. David stumped from door to door, shovelling coal. He took the floor at a labour rally and asked why their demands

could be dismissed with such contempt. There was a cheer. "Decorated over there," he hollered, "despised over here." He began to tremble. The sergeants-at-arms approached the stage. Bolster stood his ground. "Traitor," someone yelled. Someone aimed a bottle

at the accuser's skull. The chair rose to his feet and called for order. He was heckled. The vets began to stomp. A prosthetic flew at the stage. A fist fight became a brawl. A corporal began to howl "The Maple Leaf Forever." David dodged a table leg. Jean stood

up and, softly, began to sing. "Up to your waist in water, up to your eyes in slush, using the kind of language that makes the sergeant blush; who wouldn't join the army? That's what we all inquire ..." Someone finished it off: "Don't we pity the poor civilians sitting

around the fire?" That night she became *la gamine*. The following week she sang at the Veteran's Club, and the week after that David played the piano. That's how it began. On New Year's Eve, "Sophie Bonnefoy and Captain Richard Miles, CEF" wriggled out of

the pupae of Jean and David into a hall festooned with Red Ensigns and Union flags. This was the origin of Miles & Bonnefoy's *The Smile Show*, a Great War song-and-dance confection that had men weeping publicly at Saturday matinees from Moncton to Lund.

In my family the spectral great-uncles spent the century hovering in their woodsheds. A Guysborough veteran with one arm marched his family through a blizzard to see the show. When Dick pounded the piano he cried out, "Another round! Reload, you cunts!"

until he began choking. Four children looked on, horrified. "Won't last long now," said the wife, walking them to the station. The audiences roared like horses, off-key. An old hand in Vernon went straight for the oven when he got home. Second Act, Joke Four: A

young man is milking a cow on the farm. A woman, passing by, stops to watch. Dick mimes milking on a low stool. Sophie's hands move to her hips. All the other village lads are off in France. Sophie: "Boy, why aren't you at the Front?" Dick: "Because milk doesn't

come out that end!" In the summer, David pushed a broom in a synagogue. After her miscarriage, Jean adjusted the costumes and printed a new program with the old pictures. They changed the jokes, but were met with incomprehension. In 1927, the steamship

Eurana rammed the Second Narrows Bridge in Vancouver, followed by the *Norwich City* in 1928, the *Losmar* in 1930 and, later the same year, in September, a sailing vessel refitted as a log barge, the *Pacific Gatherer*, toppled the central span. That was it. The

only bridge to the North Shore was knocked out for four years. North Vancouver soon filed for bankruptcy and slid into receivership. In the 1920s, the municipality of West Vancouver had ventured an exchange of land in return for a First Narrows crossing. Two

men of commerce, one being A. J. T. (Fred) Taylor, who held the provincial franchise for the bridge, cooked up a proposal: four thousand acres of first growth west of the Capilano River in return for twenty bucks an acre, back taxes—and a way to get there.

Taylor's British connections had introduced him to the Guinness brothers, Rupert and Walter. Capital's duty is to maximize profits and minimize taxes. In 1931, the year Klee drew *Flucht vor sich*, British Pacific Properties Ltd., with the Guinnesses as principal investors, acquired the lower slopes of a mountain range and financed, at Depression wages, the eighteen-hole Capilano golf course, a school site, sewers, roads, water lines and, soaring above the Narrows, the Empire's longest suspension bridge. After a fight,

the Park Board agreed on a Stanley Park approach. For five years, prime ministerial chicanery blocked approval. Taylor held on. Imagine willing towers into the sea, and cables into the sky, fastening steel to steel, flinging fathers into the air on catwalks high

above the killer whales' annual herring spree with pails of rivets and primer. Rupert Guinness had travelled west as "Systematic Joe" Maude was approaching Baghdad, where he declared, "Our armies do not come into your cities and lands as conquerors or

enemies, but as liberators." Rupert's brief in Vancouver was to harvest lads for the Royal Navy's lower decks. His son, and the son of Walter Guinness, who'd recently entered the peerage as the first Lord Moyne, arrived in 1934 aboard a private train to inspect their

investment. At the Vancouver Club it was sockeye and whisky; everyone smiled and shook hands. Lord Moyne was cruising. Winston Churchill and his wife, Clementine, had joined him aboard his yacht *Rosaura* for a recce trip to the Levant. This was the year

that the *Velos*, a Greek vessel chartered by Yulik Braginski and his Irgun colleagues, managed to deposit 340 Polish Jews on the shores of Palestine under the noses of the Royal Navy. Within two years, the minister of Indian affairs and the Committee of the

Privy Council in Ottawa transferred a strip of the Capilano Indian Reserve No. 5 to the First Narrows Bridge Co. under section 48 of the *Indian Act*. Not a crumb of land that changed hands that day, or previously, or in the years to come, belonged to the Crown

or to the principals. "They got it for a song," said Simon Baker. The families of Xwemelch'stn had no remedy, being disenfranchised until 1960 when John Diefenbaker, embarrassed by his Commonwealth peers, amended the electoral act. Lord Moyne soon found himself reviewing the 1927 *Cinematograph Films Act* and quickly closed the loopholes enabling Columbia Pictures to shoot Quota Quickies in Victoria while preserving its British profits. That was the end of Rita Hayworth in the Willows horse

barns. It had been forty years or more since the old villages in Stanley Park were razed and the ring road graded with the bones of August Jack Khatsahlano's ancestors. He was about twenty when the engineers showed up. "We was inside this house when the

surveyors come along," he told Major Matthews, "and they chop the corner of our house when we was eating inside …" Not too long ago, close to where the surveyor sank his axe, a TV news reporter asked an elder what would happen to Vancouver if Salish title

to the land and sea were restored. "We've been here for thousands of years," he said. She began to squint. "Look at it this way," he said, "this is our Jerusalem." On July 7, 1936, shovels moved in; by the end of March, rivets were flying. In Ottawa, the Committee on

the Treatment of Enemy Aliens on the Outbreak of Hostilities was compiling names of "alien subversives" with the help of the RCMP. The new Capilano course opened to the public, as did the Golden Gate and the Pattullo Bridge across the Fraser. A good time to

be in the steel business. The monument sculptor Charles Marega had been lobbying Fred Taylor for lions couchant at the span's south end. He needed the money. "I would have preferred the lions to be in bronze or stone," he complained, "but it has to be cheap,

so they will be done in concrete, which annoys me, as I could otherwise have made both lions from one model." He died two months after the installation with eight bucks in the bank. One of the beasts is a tomb for Fred Taylor's baby shoes. What is not a tomb?

Breton published *L'amour fou* that year and shipped *Le cerveau de l'enfant* to MOMA's *Fantastic Art Dada Surrealism* show. *Time* portrayed him as a thicket, a kind of Vanaspati; he "frequently dresses entirely in green, smokes a green pipe, drinks a green liqueur and has a sound knowledge of Freudian psychology." His force field was lunar; the magus a prudish mirage. The sartorial note is an anachronistic checkmate to an infamous postwar lumber jacket. Smitten by the moment, David Gascoyne loyally

devised the poet's English voice: "our unceasing wish, growing more and more urgent from day to day, has been at all costs to avoid considering a system of thought as a refuge." Refuge as paralysis; think of Ernst's *Pietà*. But who of us could embrace or

stomach this urgent denial? Breton later on savaged Gascoyne for flirting with God. Palestinian *fedayeen* ambushed workers in March 1937 near the Jewish Colonization Association's Mesha colony in the Galilee: "a party of British police with a Lewis Gun

arrived at the scene and drove off the attackers, killing one and wounding two others." Sons are born to avenge the crimes committed on their fathers' graves. In this, all sons are brothers. "We have left undone those thinges whiche we ought to have done, and we have

done those thinges which we ought not to have done, and there is no health in us." A pistol that year began its journey to Cairo. The First Narrows crossing, its elements milled and cut in Montreal, would be 1,550 feet long with a high-tide clearance of two hundred feet,

independent of temperature or load. The company took delivery of ten thousand tons of prefabricated steel. What of David and Jean? When had their legs last found one another in the mattress pit of a cold hotel room? They'd grown into their stage names. Jean

spoke of dignity, Sophie of Picardy. Looking back, her Canadian memories were of wide streets banked with snow and pork chops in Chinese cafés at midnight. David would peer at a sandy-haired man shaving and inquire, "What are you concealing today?" How

had he come to dwell in a nation where all that mattered profoundly was concealed, where obsequiousness, acquisition by stealth and repressed insolence were the requisite virtues for citizenship? Lord Moyne, who, with his mistress, Vera Broughton, was the first to transport a live Komodo dragon home to England, concluded a new voyage and published a book, *Atlantic Circle*, with Lady Broughton's photos. "The journey of my yacht *Rosaura*," he wrote (it being a 1,536-gross-ton Newhaven–Dieppe packet), "had

certain definite objects, namely, to visit the pure-blooded Eskimos and the sites of extinct Norse settlements in southern Greenland, to collect pottery and other archaeological specimens of central American cultures, and to make zoological collections." He'd a

ship's monkey. And, was, it seems, a grave robber, a bone vivant; but who on our triumphal march is not? On May Day that year, employed and unemployed rallied at Lumberman's Arch on the midden of the old X̲wáy̲xway village site to protest the

suppression of workers' rights. Jack Lawson, the first Mac–Pap to come home, the president of the Spanish General Workers Union, and novelist and exiled anarcho-syndicalist Ramón José Sender Garcés, gave the closed-fist salute and reminded the

marchers that the abolition of workers' rights is always the first step. That month, carpenters began nailing together forms for six-inch gun batteries on Vancouver beaches. Members of the Relief Project Workers' Union still held the post office and the

art gallery when David and Jean stepped down onto the platform in late May. They'd been booked for a matinee at the Victory, a grimy vaudeville parlour weeks away from demolition. Steel-wire rope is treacherous; it expands, kinks and flips in the hot sun. The

steelworkers took their shifts at night while onshore breezes cooled the Narrows and the wire. With riptides snapping, they began pulling the strands toward the twenty-thousand-ton north anchor planted forty-four feet beneath the earth. These became the one hundred

and twenty-two strings of a lyre that seemed to float over the tides and the fish-thick sea, over whirling planets of herring—a lyre that was tuned like a Steinway grand. At night I hear the splash of scales, the heron's croak, the imperceptible chord that sings the city. Dick and Sophie lean against the wings; Sophie yanks at her skirt. Dick rubs his specs against the moth holes in his tunic. He's two days into a bout of Bell's palsy. His stump could use a new clamp. The *Attratto*, ferrying 1,400 refugees, is gliding

through the Mediterranean sans running lights, looking for a lamp on the beach. When they first played the Victory, the manager had hired a full pit orchestra—Great War vets, loyal sons of Britannia, if you believed the program. Not one, a decade later, is

alive. The fellow on the drums fell in while fishing. One was run down by his Ford. At any rate, times are tough. Dick, at the upright, glances at Mrs. Walker with her trumpet. What with her son's rheumatic fever and the old man gone, she tends to up the

tempo. She's examining her fingers. Sophie peeks through the curtain. On a raw sixteenth of December 1941, a dingy coal boat, on its way from Constanta to Palestine, anchored off Istanbul for repairs with over 780 Jewish refugees jammed into the hold. The forty-five

metre hulk had been commissioned in 1867 as a schooner-rigged steam yacht for Lord Alfred Paget. In those days, SS *Xantha* possessed the indispensible erotic charge; later names record a humbling: SS *Sea Maid*, SS *Kafireus*, SS *Esperos*, SS *Makedoniya* and,

finally, with a frayed Panamanian flag, SS *Struma*. Her top speed: six knots. The 80-h.p. engine, recently pulled from the bottom of a river, seized up as she cleared harbour; *Struma* lost way in a winter storm. A Turkish tug appeared, asking for cash; its crew

was paid in wedding rings. The Colonial Office in London instructed the Turkish authorities to return the *Struma* to the Black Sea. The Palestine quota had been met. No one was permitted ashore. In appalling circumstances, with little food, without a toilet,

the passengers appealed for help. The British ambassador in Ankara argued on behalf of the refugees: "It might be that if they reached Palestine," he wrote, "they might, despite their illegality, receive humane treatment." The colonial secretary, Lord Moyne, was furious, claiming, ingenuously, that Nazi spies were not above posing as Jewish refugees. Concessions, he said, would have "a deplorable effect throughout the Balkans in encouraging further Jews to embark on a traffic which has now been condoned by His

Majesty's Ambassador." On Christmas Eve he wrote to the Foreign Office "to urge that Turkish authorities should be asked to send the ship back to the Black Sea, as they originally proposed." For two months the Turks resisted. After miscarrying, a woman

went ashore. Nine others escaped. Visas to Palestine were offered to seventy children; the deal collapsed when Turkey refused to let them travel overland. Bitter winds lashed the decks. On February 23, the *Struma* was towed back through the Bosphorus into

the Black Sea and cut loose ten kilometres from shore. It's reported that people along the route saw signs hung out in English and Hebrew that read SAVE US. The next day the ship was blown to smithereens by a torpedo from Soviet sub SC-213. One man lived,

clinging to wreckage as his fellow passengers succumbed to hypothermia. The official history records that three of the Soviet submariners "demonstrated exemplary courage in the action." *Struma, Struma, Struma.* Lord Moyne became deputy resident minister

of state for Persia, Africa and the Middle East. Rommel was hunkered down in El Alamein. In New York, Breton was broadcasting over the Voice of America from translations by Marc Chagall's son-in-law. Anyone knows that you can't trust British

foreign policy. All war is civil war; best take matters into your own hands. Lord Moyne contributed a foreword to Ronald McIntyre's *Films Without Make-Up*, saluting the courage of cameramen in North Africa. He was appointed resident minister in

Cairo. Egged on by Churchill, he'd become intrigued by partition as an exit strategy with benefits. Churchill had toyed with arming Jewish settlers in Palestine to free up British, Australian and New Zealand troops for Egypt. He told Chaim Weizmann, now's the time to visit my friend Moyne. On the morning of November 6, 1944, Eliyahu Bet-Zuri, twenty-two, and Eliyahu Hakim, seventeen, members of Lehi, hid outside Moyne's residence on Hassan Sabry Street with handguns. Taking their cue from the IRA, they ambushed his

car as it was returning for lunch. Lance Corporal Fuller, the driver, was shot at close range. Hakim fired three rounds through an open window at Moyne who asked, before losing consciousness, "When will the doctor arrive?" Attended by King Farouk's

physician, Walter Guinness did not last the night. Hakim and Bet-Zuri fled on bikes and were caught on Fouad al-Awal Bridge. In prison they asked for Kipling's poems. When their executions were delayed, Churchill intervened. In red burlap they were blindfolded

and hanged in Cairo that March. In 1975 their remains were exchanged for twenty prisoners from Sinai and Gaza and buried on Mount Herzl with military honours. Their faces appeared on Israeli stamps in 1982. A man in a green suit enters the Victory. He's

sweating, and sits alone, placing his hat in his pipe. Sophie turns to Dick. He extends his leg, and she begins. "She is watching by the poplars, Colinette with the sea-blue eyes; she is watching and longing and waiting, where the long white roadway lies ..." David

looks up, and there is Jean. There are ducks on the water. Walter Guinness never did set eyes on the lyre that vaults the Narrows, the swooping bride of time. Wherever we are, every night's a wedding night. The tide is constant, regenerating the world's bones.

who took you in

after the boarding house burned to the curb in Deseronto
upstream in scrub cedar, anticipating betrayal
with the bicycle gone, doors locked and rain setting in
when your lungs ripped like old curtains
with your thought a slurry
as the bus pulled out and the platform went dark
and the lights along the border crashed
after the car struck
with garrisons on every corner
when a shovel was your mother
when your people refused to hide you
when you knocked on the cathedral door
and the tanker ran aground
when the torpedo struck
when they found someone to blame
when the blood resembled yours
when the stick snapped
when you stepped before the throne

if you ask would i join you in the plum forest
sleep beside you, call you comrade
with the scent of leaves at night beneath our heads
and Pan the last god standing
i'd say yes

South Sl

next
door's
kittens

scaled
the
screen

door
in
the

dark
pantry
but

it's
a
bear's

nose
pressing
in

Reckoning

I give in. I cave out. I promise. I *puh*. I give out. I give. I cave in.

o

Three hundred and ninety-six moons since I drove up the Fish Lake Road to begin
        a reckoning,
carrying your cracked hearts home from the honey light of Knutsford
to claim that cold, damp ticking in a resentful northern shire.
My heart swims, it's a straw mushroom, a tommy cod, and on the day she made a
        harvest basket of
her skirt—there were asps, wasps, aspen, rashes, ruts, rattles by that sea, a spinnaker in
        a pinafore—
it was a gets, guest, I was a gust, no, wattles, waffles, I'm a little rusty, but
I picture you, the tall, and stout, the crush of, bunch of, crash of, grass beneath your
        swish, swish through
the hayfield, spent, distracted by snakes in the cottonwoods.

o

Uncoupled from your convoy, heavy with duty, pistons banging, stokers delirious
        with heat,
pitching, shuddering, *Star Weeklies* down the front, icicles in the fo'c'sle, tuned to sleet:
MAY DAY, MAY DAY, MAY DAY.

o

Imagine no apocalypse.
What then?
You vanish.
That's it.
Fish will return
land will rise, fall
merlins will take sparrows on
the blackberries.

Happiness is a chuckling river in which you are
a snowflake. The new road to the compound—they'll scrape
moss from the roof and replumb the latrines—
will be a hurricane of hardy hibiscus with functional bike islands.
Award-winning traffic lights will be installed.
Sniff the rugosa, watch your pinkies.
Akhmatova observed "grilled scolopendras on stones,"
this in 1913 when you'd hear God breathing
on the party line.

And what of that huge, supine, colon-shaped multipede on the edge of the Bering Sea
that pulls itself along with its elbows until it spots a man hunting?
It flings its legs into the air, and from a distance the waving resembles a party of
foragers in need—perhaps a man is down, a child is sick, a girl is
giving birth. The solitary hunter's heart goes out to that family.
He drops his rifle and runs sobbing through the mud
and scrub
to be snatched up by racks of polluted teeth.
But his fate is not the world's.
The world is fateless.

What exists is not as you imagine it, and
is indestructible.

o

Why is your neighbourhood
short of pyramids?

A dearth of slaves,
that's why.

Slaves are to monumental beauty
as teeth are to a wolverine.
Without slaves, you're less than an atom
in a thistle's sap.

Attention, Bataille's bronze dong!
Slaves are the silent dongs of majesty.

o

The Fowlers of Guernsey   major *&* minor
Henry and Francis   reflector *&* shiner
a year of weeks in yards away
from the other's vestibule.
Frank did the tomatoes. Henry, his senior, shaved
and slaved in his shade, as he saw it,
preparing shadow barracks.
Hardy rootstock in stone cots, grateful
for a day-old paper, they set sail with Lucian of

Samosata who begins ΛΗΘΩΝ ΔΙΗΓΗΜΑΤΩΝ
(*A True Story*) thusly:

> *I think I can escape the censure of the world by*
> *my own admission that I'm not telling a word of truth.*

Said Henry, "I am the most unliterary person that ever
posed as an expert on how to write." He ran and swam
each morning until seventy.

Do you call this a masquerade?
Something was ending.
Modern English Usage
arrived in 1926.

In two houses.
In two books.
In two skins.
Why?

A sentence fell off the table at the Spotted Spigot
A man carried the beating heart and
wings with trembling eyes into the back.
"Almost unheard of," he said.

For John Hicks

what do they fear?

that they'll never
return?

that they'll never
want to?

Les prisonniers ont le droit de s'enfuir

For Viviane Houle & Stefan Smulovitz

Is there a higher law
a holy law
in heaven, or
on earth?

"... and you, so near to your demise?"

+

Dans les marches de Lorraine,
dans le bois chesnu,
sous l'arbre des fées,
à côté de Crotoy …

    "La clarté vient au nom de la voix."

Dans les champs de Domremy,
dans le jardin de sa père,
en été, à midi, Catherine,
Marguerite, un archange …

    "La clarté vient au nom de la voix."

At Chinon and Orléans,
in the forest of Patay,
at the siege of Saint-Pierre,
in the arrow at Rouvray …

    "Avant, gentil duc, à l'assault."

+

"*Et ton état?*"
"And your encounter?"

"Grace, when in God's arms.
 Grief, should He refuse me."

"*... men are sometimes hanged for telling the truth.*"

"*Je actens à Dieu,
 mon créatur, de tout:
 je l'ayme
 de tout mon cuer.*"

+

*"la clarté vient
au nom de la voix"
la clarté*

*"cette voix
est belle et douce et humble"
"la clarté vient
au nom de la voix"
la voix*

*"je les entends tres bien
bon et beau
belle et douce et humble"*

*"si je n'y suis
Dieu m'y mette
et
si j'y suis
Dieu m'y tienne
la voix"*

"the light enters in the name of the voice"

+

I sail across the green earth,
over industrial water,
His voice is in the sedges,
my Lord in the hedges,
Jehanne on the edges,

and under the hawk's dream
the Lady's Tree hung
with God's tongues.

   Anadraxonora.
   Biladrido.
   Oonapilladrola.

Seigneur, Seigneur,
Great Bear,
I bear your glory;
hear me,
steer me.

+

Hail Mary.
Gale Mary.
Rain Mary.
Snow Mary.
Sleet Mary.
Squall Mary.
Fog Mary.
Wind Mary.
Wave Mary.
Hale Mary.
Grail Mary.
Hire Mary.
Fire Mary.
Him Mary.
Hymn Mary.
Him Mary.
Him.

> *Mes voix, où sont*
> *mes voix?*

I'm burning!

That shape I see?
Who can that shadow be?

A man without wings.

What is a man
without wings?

+

This hold on life
is slight.
This grip on this hold on life
is slight.
This grasp on this grip on this hold on life
is slight.
This clutch on this grasp on this grip on this hold on life
is slight.
This clasp on this clutch on this grasp on this grip on this hold on life
is slight.
This choke on this clasp on this clutch on this grasp on this grip on this hold on life is slight.
Is light. Is slight.
This claw on this choke on this clasp on this clutch on this grasp on this grip on this hold on life is slight.
Is light.
Is light.
This hook on this claw on this choke on this clasp on this clutch on this grasp on this grip on this hold on life is ...

... Your voice

in the Lady's tree.

+

Why fear a woman
in love with her Lord?

Why burn a woman
in love with her Lord?

    Où sont mes voix?

You ask what love
has taught me?
If you free a nation from slavery,
it will rise up
and bind you down.

Seigneur, cowards are
in Your image made.

    Où sont mes voix?

Interrupting harness!

Extraordinary rendition!

I seek no reprieve.

    What is a woman without wings?

+

Is there a law
within the law
a truth within
the lie?

      "Les prisonniers ont le droit de s'enfuir."

Is the prison
within the prison
the prison
of the eye?

      "The light enters in the name of the voice."

"Never doubt.
When God pleases,
the hour
is nigh."

      "As long as I live, I will never abandon you."

+

Stefan Smulovitz's luminous score for Carl Dreyer's 1928 silent film *The Passion of Joan of Arc* was first performed on January 28, 2010, at Christ Church Cathedral in Vancouver, British Columbia, by the Eye of Newt Ensemble, thanks to a commission from the PuSh International Performing Arts Festival, with support from the British Columbia Arts Council, and presented with the Vancouver 2010 Cultural Olympiad. The words on these pages, some taken from the transcripts of Joan's trial, and now slightly revised, were lifted into song by Viviane Houle.

COMPOSER: Stefan Smulovitz
VOICE: Viviane Houle
TRUMPET: J. P. Carter, John Korsrud
TROMBONE: Jeremy Berkman
VIOLIN: Rebecca Whitling, Cam Wilson
VIOLA: Reg Quiring
CELLO: Peggy Lee
PERCUSSION: Daniel Tones
PIPE ORGAN: Michael Murray
CONDUCTOR: Giorgio Magnanensi

Many thanks to Stefan Smulovitz, Viviane Houle
and Norman Armour of the PuSh Festival.

Peace Banged on My Door

Peace banged on my door
cheeks rosy as Kandahar.
I was gutting a rabbit
named Lou, for stew.

I sang, as I boned, "Madeleine Muldoon"
then "The Boy Pierced by Spears,"
and turned the turnips on. Old Lou'd
carried a torch for tarragon.

I barked out "The Seal Wife's Gown"
and the knocking resumed.
Eyes red, throat sore,
Peace strode in with a tomb.

"I've had it. I tried," he cried. "No more."
We bellowed out "The Tinker of Wilfred's Snout"
and "The Ten-Hour Hanging."
I spooned the velouté out.

Solemn as granite he downed a carrot.
He torched the crème brûlée.
We soared on the chorus of
"The Grim Quarry of Glee!"

Herman Melville at the Morning Star

> *... to search out the things which have been hidden since the creation of*
> *this wondrous world, or seen only by the naked Indian, who has, for*
> *unknown ages, dwelt in the gorgeous but melancholy wilderness.*
> JOHN JAMES AUDUBON, "The Raven"
> *The Birds of America*, Vol. 4

> *Dans les nacelles de l'enclume*
> *Vit le poète solitaire*
> *Grande brouette des marécages.*
> RENÉ CHAR, "Poètes"

Any ketch longs for landfall.
When a sail appears on the streaking sea
what is your obligation?

The "Matt Damon's back" in the window is vacant. Make that "table"
as in "delay" for "picture." Snowflakes, fat as sugar packets.
The wings of intention render to a spine.
Flenser, you ask, why are we here?

> *I beg leave to congratulate you upon the honor of having been a whale-*
> *hunter in your time.*
> HERMAN MELVILLE, June 22, 1886

Its claws are cooper's bands.
Audubon's strange little butler in britches is fretful,
an angel
abandoned by its Lord.

He watches as it stoops to take a rooster,
then bags his specimen.

> *It proved a young male, such as you see, kind reader, represented in the*
> *Plate, pursuing a lovely Blue-bird nearly exhausted. The Cock was also*
> *dead; its breast was torn, and its neck pierced in several places by the*
> *sharp claws of the Hawk.*
> JOHN JAMES AUDUBON, "Cooper's Hawk"
> *The Birds of America*, Vol. 1

He's seen pigeons torn helplessly from the blue;
tableaux unsuited to art's
masquerade.

The French poet showed up like the carcass of something
encountered after two weeks at sea,
his forenoon disintegrating,
glum as a pipsqueak.

In Melville's hand, a packet of sugar.
His fingers read the crimps.
He'd take an eighty-knot headwind over California.
Inside may crave the triumph of outside,
though what's sprung
is irretrievable.

What steers our little skiff
across the dark bight?

The things that have been hidden.

He sits in the window of the Morning Star Café on Ninth Avenue
with a hyena, a manatee and a thylacine
intent on an omelette of his own devising.

A waiter douses the manatee with a jug of water
though chlorine stings
and irritates its desiccated skin.
The thylacine compresses its tail.
A jackal was eaten overnight.

Melville's gloomy. "The population inside me," he growls, "is fed up."

Hyena: "My people had the good fortune not to fall from the sky. They came from
fire. Bacon … mounds of it!"

The thylacine, with a snap of its long tail: "Mine too."

The sea cow grunts. "You familiar with *Manitou*, the word *Manitou*?" it asks.

Melville was acquainted with the Wampanoag, the Nantucket and the Pennacook.

"No relation," says the manatee.

For a moment it seemed to laugh, though its mouth, thinks Melville,
was not made for laughing. Nor is the menu made to please
a transitional mammal designed for intertidal grazing.
The waiter tosses on two tumblers of water.

He'd glimpsed the Frenchman on West Fifty-Sixth lugging bags into his sad building.
What word ending in "orn" are we not?

"I was carrying deepest darkness in myself."

Melville rotates the sugar packet.
Is pride the constant?
He's pitted by his grief.

At Nootka: Stellar's jays
before the wreck at
Kamchatka.

"Claws strong, arched, compressed, sharp."

He's weary of these animals and their noses.
They can't sit still.
They lick everything.

A battered omelette arrives, and champagne buckets of bacon.
His tablemates fall to bragging and coarse humour.
The manatee bellows for lubrication.
Melville broods.
The hour of plenitude is the hour of danger.
A bulldog in a cerulean cardigan marches by without.
"That reminds me …," says hyena.
The thylacine springs three snouts closer to the door.

The light is opened. The Frenchman
picks a crumb off his green jacket
and unwraps a parcel in a miserable
room in the new world.

He can't believe his luck.
In his hand, the sign Matta's after.
Cottonwood to combat the word.

The packet crackles in his fingers. Melville's glad
the TV's off. Those torsos of human pudding,
small, fierce men pinned to noseblood-streaked mats
as their partners pull on the ropes:
temptation.

Hyena lunges at thylacine, who flees.
The manatee has lost consciousness. Melville calls the waiter
and rips open the sugar.
In millions of years this animal will bubble up as a reason for a war.
The cup is cold.
The waiter hands him the bill and goes for the newsstand guys next door.
Melville dips napkins in his glass and mops the panting hide.

He flips his omelette to see what's underneath.
The news guys and two cops in chartreuse jackets
clasp their arms and slide them under
the nodding beast. Melville pushes against the animal with his shoulder
and the men heave it out the door.
A time of mendacity, he thinks, of deceit
burnished to a virtue in a stricken nation.
Outside, the manatee's being crushed into a cruiser. Inside, the public
purse is being burgled for subsidy and profit.
He'd charted alpha and omega.
Ishmael's tale is told in the glow of a flat-wick burner.
Oil Springs, Titusville: the new Nantuckets,
altars roaring in the dark.

The cruiser's gone, a blizzard
obscures the scaffolding. A few grains of sugar on the table,
yellow hairs on the chair, the bill.
He's alone. His body has
its own purpose now.

The Frenchman's flat? Demolished.
Across the way, with Duchamp,
where he presented his mane
to a woman "draped in blue shadows?"
Torn down.

Melville tugs at his hoodie.
The snow's sticking to pigeons.
What will not be bent?

A man watching cries out, "I never give up.
That's why I keep on going."

I fear my words
won't bear the light.

Unobtrusive wormhole in margins of first gathering

what do you want from me
after all these years? I told you
I would never call you *master*.

An Inauguration, April 15, 2009

who's asked
who's asked to
who's asked to speak for
who is asked to speak for
who's asked to speak for
who is asked to
is asked for
who's asked for
who's asked to
who's asked to speak for
is asked to speak
asks to speak for who
asks to speak for
asks to speak for who
is not
is not asked
is not asked to
is not asked to speak for
is not asked to speak for who
is not asked to speak for
whose shoes are
whose shoes are
whose shoes are asked for
whose shoes are whose
who's who is who
who's who is asked for
whose whose
whose whose
who's who
who's who
who's not is not who's who

who's not is not who's whose
whose shoes
whose whos
who's asked for
whose whos
whose whos are
who's whose is
whose whose is whose who
whose who
who's whose
who's whose is whose who
who's who
who's who
who's asked for
whose shoes
whose shoes
whose shoes are
whose shoes are asked for
whose shoes
who's whos
who's who?

first performed by Viviane Houle at Fluevog Shoes, Vancouver

The Laurel
For Daphne Guernsey

How the daughter of Ladon, that celebrated river, hated the works
of marriage and how the Nymphe became a tree with inspired
whispers; she escaped the bed of Phoibos but she crowned his hair
with prophetic clusters.
NONNUS, *Dionysiaca*

Perhaps we'll meet again in a better world.
RICHARD STRAUSS to Clemens Krauss, August 1944

Without one, one is not one. Is one? Is one one? Is one who is not one not one but is one
who is no one one? To be one, and not one, is to be one not being no one. But without

one, one is no one, is one not? One is, and one is not. Why be one? To be one and not no
one is to be one. If a nation is one. If a nation is one, one is or is not one, but one is not

no one. No one is no one. She knew. The great-aunt Daphne, who was never one, was
one not not being no one, with the bearing of an imperilled one who'd been a spared

one. Who's one, who's one's foe, pray? Bear down. What does it profit one to bear down,
or to forgive? What's forgiveness but one's claim on future considerations? Bellow to

Faulkner, peevishly: no quarter for that "crank." "The creek," she said, "you can't. Even
before us you couldn't. Daddy said don't drink it." See the shining majuscules forming

and reforming in the eddies. The occupation bore down without mercy, the first wave
mineral, epidermal. Seams jutted out of the hills like dried blood. Probe a vein, poke a

hole. Scavengers tore from shaft to shaft, spewing pyrites, blasting craters.
Dormant nursery colonies, exposed and teeming with pyrite bacteria—*extremophiles*—

oxidized, leeching arsenic into the water table as soluble acid sulphides. Scorched earth, scorched water. No one was watching but Indians and that was no one. The valley was

her Jerusalem. A Chinese cook, an impatient mother, an indulgent father and sheep. A horse named Blackie. At sixteen, a mistress of dogs and stallions. In the barn at White

Lake she endured the cycles of temporary love with disposable ruminants. In May the Osoyoos women and kids pitched tents in the greasewood with shovels and Saskatoon-

berry sticks for prying out roots. In June, the old man drove his ewes up onto the mountain. On fall nights flammulated owls, none plumper than a rock rose bulb, fled

the ponderosas for Mexico. What was the answer to the six-word clue in the family crossword? Bear down. The old man sold the ranch in 1944. Poetry and war are like a

mouth with a toothpick. That year François Mauriac hijacked a paean to the resistance poets to pick at the *surréaliste* scab and to nail a provincial plank against *les portes du*

merveilleux. "That music they'd invented for their own private intoxication," he charged, "that turbid stream became suddenly clear, and they were able to distribute its waters to

a people perishing of thirst." She'd have approved, though she'd no time for "the people." She'd have taken the measure of Aragon's lines from *Saint-Pol-Roux ou l'espoir*: "The

secret wounds of my country are the deepest. The wounds of which one does not speak." Péret, in Mexico, fuming, accused his old comrades of sermonizing from a "false

witness box" in a craven bid for posterity. The nation, like all institutions, is an abattoir. At its most endearing it bears the closest scrutiny. Beware the blue flame of purification;

the unspeakable builds nests where crows are scarce. In the first month of the Great War, fifty thousand patriotic poems a day arrived in the mailrooms of Berlin's dailies.

As late as 1917 Thomas Mann believed war would lead Europe to become "simple and graceful" and "filled with disgust for its former negro-like craving for pleasure and the

ostentatiousness of civilisation ..." When will the state martyr itself for its citizens? How does trust imperil one? Bear down. Men should not cross gods. In Richard Strauss's

Bukolische Tragödie, Daphne, a nymph lives for hunting; Ovid is smitten by her floating hair in the sacred grove. One evening she and Leukippos, his gender concealed, dawdle

in the moss with their hounds, chatting like sisters. Lovesick Phoebus Apollo's flaming dart—a lightning bolt—makes quick work of his rival: a woman one moment, a man the

next, a cinder soon after. Lucky Leukippos, your agony's ended. "Sorrow-stricken Daphne!" Apollo has butchered your consolation. Now, Apollo's options are two: sex or

incineration, or sex and incineration. Chaste as ivory, Daphne resists. "*Du ewiger Träumer.*" The dreamer's law is unsparing. He is world unhappy. "Daddy had a gold

mine." Each year, to tend his dream, she drove to Hedley and chucked in a couple of dynamite sticks. Under the lark-blue sky, kicking up alkali dust, beneath a buffalo robe

in an open car on a starry night, she adored the beast whose alphabet was her landscape. "*Ich komme, ich komme, Grünende Brüder ...*" What was Daphne to the G.I. who found an

old guy in the rubble exclaiming, "I am the composer of *Rosenkavalier* and *Salome*?" But when the occupiers paid a formal visit he played the final F-sharp major melody from

Daphne—"the *Walküre* magic fire music with different notes," he'd told his librettist. *Eine kleine Übereinkunft* with *der Führer* likely spared his family and bought him time.

And if he'd taken a stand? A state's legitimacy exists as long as one sanctions it. Can one who's not one be one? Stefan Zweig's books were stripped by students from the

National Library and torched in the Berlin Opernplatz on a May night in 1933 to martial anthems and the squawks of sausage hawkers. Heaving *Totem und Tabu* into the

bonfire, a functionary sang out, "Against the soul-destroying glorification of the instinctual life, for the nobility of the human soul!" Tailed by Nazis, Zweig turned down

the libretto for Strauss's next opera. The composer was furious. "Your letter of the 15th drives me to despair! This Jewish obstinacy!" When Strauss stood up for Zweig in 1935,

Goebbels removed him as head of the German *Reichsmusikkammer*. He'd never liked him anyway. Strauss complained to Hitler. No reply. Within weeks the Panzer IV was in

clandestine production in Magdeburg with a 75 mm howitzer and leaf-spring double-bogie suspension. Daphne was seven. "I belong to a nation of 'servants and waiters',"

fumed Strauss, "and almost envy the racially persecuted Stefan Zweig." He had no patience for "the everyday," he said, "it doesn't really suit me." He was accused of

"feminine voluptuousness." "Daddy," she said, "was friendly with the Indians. He knew the chief. When there was trouble he'd bail out the sons." Or was it the other way

around? "Some nights, I'd hear hooves in the yard. There'd be signs next morning in the barn." Strauss set his heart to *Daphne* after conducting his "Olympic Hymn" for three thousand voices at the Berlin summer Games. ("I, the out-spoken enemy and despiser of all sport!") Dressed in gleaming white, the chorus had belted out the "Horst Wessel Song"

as Hitler entered the stadium. *Daphne* was a notion of the new librettist, Joseph Gregor. Gentiles, apparently, could also be obstinate; Strauss complained to Zweig of "words

heaped upon words." Karl Böhm led the premiere in Dresden in October 1938 and got a kiss from Strauss's wife, Pauline. The Nazis began intimidating Alice, her daughter-in-

law, warning that divorce was the family's only guarantee of security. Strauss refused. Alice was later placed under house arrest; when her family was sent to Theresienstadt,

Strauss drove to the camp to demand their release. He was sent away. *Daphne* was revived in Munich in 1942 with the composer conducting for the last time in his life and

bombs screaming into the streets. During carnival week in Brazil, Zweig and his wife had swallowed Veronal. They were found on their bed, fully dressed, holding hands,

with their dog alive at their feet. His note read, "All too impatient, I am going on alone." The opera houses were pulverized one by one: Dresden, Weimar, Vienna, the *Staatsoper*

Munich in 1943. Strauss to his biographer Willi Schuh: "This is the greatest catastrophe of my life, for which there can be no consolation." The old man was inclined to mischief.

He'd show a perky herd in the morning, shake on a deal, but when the truck pulled away there'd be unanticipated substitutions. A misunderstanding? Perhaps. Wily wool-puller.

One's reminded of a god. And gullibility's anguish invites pecking. Who's one to one who's not one? Who's not one to one who is? "Daddy compartmentalized." "He could be very sociable; that was just an act." For whom? "He was a great flirt." A nanny was fired for moral laxity. Vengeful seigneur. When his only son hit puberty, he dispatched him to

the Royal Navy. He took up with a young woman our family called the Whore. Her mother. In his boots and spurs the old boy was a sorry and grateful Apollo. Pauline

Strauss-de Ahna, known to the shrews of Munich as the Shrew of Munich, loved *Daphne* best of all. Beside the River Ladon, Gaea's peerless daughter, soul sister to

Artemis, clear-eyed Daphne brings her hounds to heel at the edge of the grove. The sky darkens. Tusky gentlemen scoot into the hills. She burns with green fire. Enter the

magnificent god. At the sound of thunder and the piercing of the sky, at his fiery descent and lunge, she withdraws, refuses. The glory of her voice moves the omnipotent

one. He relents. Her limbs drill into the earth. From her toes tendrils grow, then roots, her arms spiral upward as lustrous branches, leaves burst forth and berries the colour of

her eyes. She greens into fragrant heartwood. The shimmering mist of language clears. A new tree glows in the forest. Thus did she resist the amorous god and the Law for the

Protection of German Blood and German Honour. "*Unsterblicher Liebe*" rises in ecstatic chords. "Mortals ... brothers ... make me a symbol of love never ending ..." The sublime

transformation ends with five pounds of bacon and an oboe in three-four time on a rainy night in March, alone and frightened in a house where she was the only one. Once, in a

curtain of sleet, I climbed her steps to describe a half-sister's funeral to which she'd not been invited. She poured four tumblers of whisky. I later found libertarian tracts from a conspiracy theorist (the Jews again) who'd tried to recruit her for an anti-Trudeau insurrection. One day she phoned. "Come. *Now*." She rushed me to a closet and began

pulling out suits. "Try this. Take this." Too small, too old, too shiny. "Take something, anything. Something must fit." Ignorant and slow, I fiddled with a sweater. Then: "My

God, Daphne, these are your husband's, aren't they?" How long had it been? Strauss in his last years returned often to that final theme. "*Unsterblicher Liebe*." On his deathbed,

confiding to his beloved Alice, he recalled music written sixty years before: "Dying is just as I composed it in *Tod und Verklärung*." Welcome home, golden-crowned daughter.

Laurel's evening gleams. You were defiant, and submitted to no one. Dignity you gleaned from the old man, and the romancing of calamity. You were not one who knelt,

or courted mercy, or bayed at altars to flatter a bellowing god. You did the *Androsace lanuginosa* and were no one's beloved. You were one, but not a spared one. You were a

divided one. Rattle, beak, petal, spine; you were fierce, multiple, resolute. And how quickly it all went, with harrowing, predictable precision. Scrim followed scrim followed

scrim—then the curtain. Two British steam locomotives were plated with your name: one, an unsuperheated 4-4-0 in the Precursor class on the London, Midland and

Scottish line, the other a 0-6-0T engine that ran on the Shropshire and Montgomeryshire. Built in 1872, it was one of the "Terriers," scrapped when you were five. Coal fires drove

their wheels, shooting sparks against black hills. I think of Rilke's dark laurel, pressed against the sky, how it animates a world the will longs to pierce with meaning, as the bow seeks to pierce the boar, and the tenderness with which the eyes turn aside. My tenderness, I admit, was wanting. Gods *are* terriers, beautiful and irresistible. The owls

return when the bitterroot blooms—*inmitten dieser sonnenatmenden Erde*—high in the ponderosas. "*Selige Vögel, Wohnet in mir ...*" You'll hear a sound as they sleep. *Daphne.*

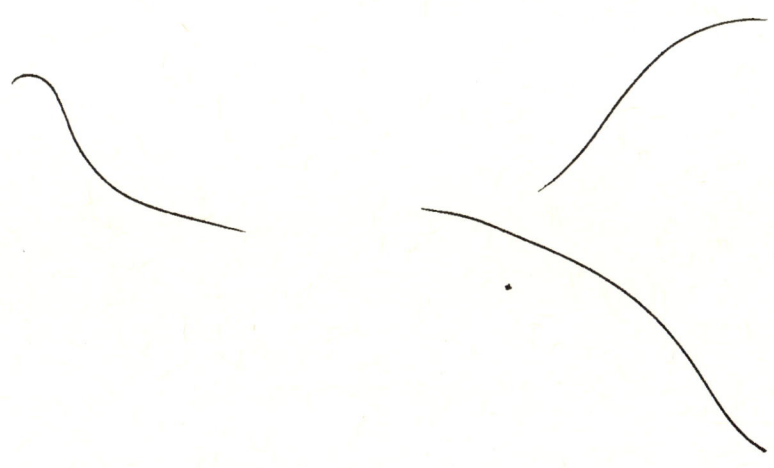

What are you waiting for?
The flag in the quince
is a bird calling, "*Marco*."
Occasionally a naked person
passes the mirror. The cedar fills up
with herons. Blossoms drop into a wagon
parked outside an abandoned cinema.
Lead breaks when I write I.

Listening in bed to finches
is a luxury. One by one
my friends are going. They
struggle, and then
the mysterious gathering-in
occurs. They don't need me now.
Their minds have found what
they always knew they'd find.

The War in Asia

"Everyone was in good humour,
    even the boys who spent the whole day in the sun
    and the next day put a bullet through their brains."

shame

i see george bowering everywhere i go
he has been here before me
and i'm grateful for
he has made me

a place to live in
as for those old earle birneys
i've ignored
on the shelf at macleod's

i'm more ashamed
of an encounter
in the provincial
museum

forty years ago
when i tapped
him on the shoulder
and asked if

we could talk
sit down, he said,
grinning
gee, i thought

earle birney,
alone with
his bag
in a museum

cafeteria
is it really you?
i'm thrilled, sir,
to meet you

it appeared
to make
his poet's
heart sing

he was smiling
like a border collie
please tell me, i said, all about
malcolm lowry

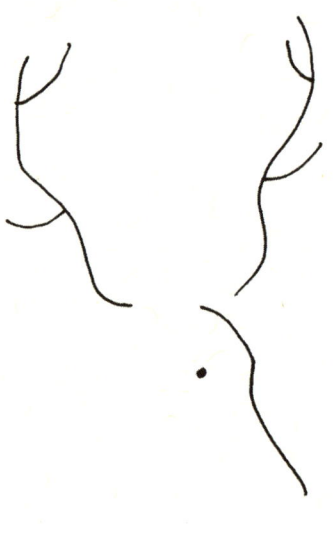

The Grenade
For Kythé Mackenzie (1917–2010)

My mother spoke to the toast.
"You haven't changed," she said,
"I get nothing from you,
* after all these years."*

I

The afternoon swarms
    with glinting things
        she patrols. Cosmos,

cornflowers, ivory
    flags. She's not
        one for roses.

Rose campion, yes,
    & lamb's ears,
        like glowing

broomwood coals.
    A classmate,
        eighty years on,

"She was the prettiest ..."
    Straw-white bangs
        on the grass court,

struck on the bean
    while turning
        cartwheels

by a cricket ball.
    A limb split in the front
        yard when a lady's name

blew through; told
                of the axe murder
                                she registered no surprise.

"Keep picking *&* your face
                will cave in," she said.
                                Gassing up the Chev

in North Dakota, we
                encountered dramatic
                                proof. On the day

les gueules cassées broke
                ranks, she emerged
                                in an orchard.

Her mother was confined
                for two weeks. When
                                her father came home

she screamed blue
                murder. You're a girl,
                                a girl, a girl, then

for years
                you smell of
                                urine and cloves.

2

I don't want help.
       Our oars synched up
              on Williams Lake

when two dragonflies
       flew by, fused.
              The girl said, "Do

you know what
       they're doing?"
              Dying, perhaps?

Mysterious & alarming
       in the bathtub,
              my mother's round eyes.

They must hide
       in her shirt.
              She smiled.

It was better
       than being tossed
              a bag of margarine

to punch on the
       kitchen floor.
              We treaded water.

In the box, a green disk,
      the "Tennessee Waltz."
           She took in typing,

dried wishbones,
      fried puffballs.
           When Lukey with

the dimpled arms
      soaked haddock
           we sang "Lukey's Boat."

We got back to the tent
      with the mouldy loaf;
           a farmer was hauling

our Chev out of
      quicksand
           on top of

Old Smokey.
      A boy died of
           goofballs on

the Herring Cove Road.
      A hurricane tore a gash
           in the road, her photo

family in the trunk
      turned into porridge.
           Men rushed out

with flashlights.
    I saw the girl
        with snakes

in her shirt
    conducting
        the storm.

My mother wept.
    Frugality, and
        keeping your

head down,
    unlike our Catholic
        cousins who grew

beautiful with
    long necks
        and .303s

in the basilica
    basement,
        said my dad.

3
My father sang
     to his razor, "I've got
          the horse right here ..."

It was like hearing
     the Heart of the Sky
          making the world.

Her mind was departure,
     going home. She did not
          sing. Brown paper

packets of fisherman's
     socks arrived at Christmas
          from *Scotland*.

I believed they were
     pulled off a man
          who'd drowned at sea.

"I brought my sorrow with me,"
     she said in the dream.
          If she bent over

at the mess, or at home,
     there were naval officers
          with rum and beards.

She held her tongue.
     And had no antidote
         for the monkey bite

so I waited to die.
     No one blamed
         the British submariners.

After all, it wasn't
     the Reds, it was us
         hicks they were

keeping an eye on.
     And she got it,
         she understood

long before her
     husband did. *They*
         were farming *us*.

Britannia's spear was
     a bloodsucker's siphon.
         My mother began to build

a nation in opposition,
     a nation of something
         other than arse licking.

And she was slapped down.
　　Ottawa slapped her down,
　　　　Halifax slapped her down,

the Navy slapped her down,
　　her family slapped her down.
　　　　We all slapped her down.

4
What Thoreau's crush infers
    about the frog in his hat,
        she'd have liked. Duchamp too.

Never lost a card game, never
    pretended to. Immune to
        charmers: Prince Philip,

Monty, Mountbatten,
    the admiral, the padre,
        the commodore,

the wife Tootie and
    her poodle, the minister,
        the deputy, the attaché,

the doctor who ate
    raw onion sandwiches,
        the bishop at All Saints,

filthy brutes all.
    With its royal blue
        covers and two little

princesses in diadems,
    the scrapbook was a
        control tower.

Much later,
     David Niven
          rounded the corner

into Grosvenor Square.
     She consorted with
          the enemy that day.

5
Seeing pines
     for the unseen.
          Knowing hedges

its bets, advances
     an ideal, hatches
          vivid raptures

& names them
     Unknowable.
          "How?" she asks.

"How do you know?"
     Then, Thumper—
          pace Tom Paine:

"If you can't say
     anything nice,
          don't say anything

at all." Standard
     issue blue and
          white. Blue Willow

in the bank
     at Breezy Bay,
          pagodas, fishing

poles and bridges.
      Liz ran up the road
           to find an egg

in a hole. Egg,
      hole, temple,
           tiny fishermen,

a sampan's pole.
      Homes known
           Unknown.

[A line] does not illustrate. It is the sensation of its own realization.
                                  CY TWOMBLY, "Signs," 1957

6
To what could
         she be true? In
                  whom could she trust?

The headmistress's
         brother turning
                  down a side road?

Lies were not
         less so for being
                  welcome. Her

friend Shirley's
         first paying job
                  was at an Indian

school upcountry.
         Later, in the Blitz,
                  the two of them

underground
         tracking Junkers 88s,
                  living like nuns

with breasts.
    Éluard, in Paris, writing,
        "Sur les merveilles des nuits,

Sur le pain blanc des journées ..."
    I is for Invisible.
        War, she discovers,

is a collaboration
    between foes
        for the perpetuation

of inequity,
    the temporary
        transfer of wealth,

and the indefinite
    deferral of justice.
        Pick a new street

each morning,
    an unexpected
        thoroughfare.

You'll be followed.
    Walk into
        the earth.

Day becomes other,
    as moonlight
        becomes ardent you.

7
The moon is no lamb.
     Forests soar on
          unfulfilled desire.

She shed sorrow
     after sorrow
          until she shed

no more. Those she
     she loved were
          stolen from her

one by one.
     "I want no
          history," she said.

"Don't ask me
     anything." Moults
          & phantom moults.

The maternal
     exoskeleton, brittle;
          in battle adamant.

The weeping, then
     the assassination of
          what wept. Then,

the ploughing on,
      her mother called it,
            the years of spite

and indignation.
      How does a girl
            become a grenade?

8

Being in not being,
      or "the motions."
            She haunted

who she'd been.
      Sycamore Mother,
            I was the little

stick king
      tugging at
            each word's tit.

Your mother tongue
      your mother's tongue,
            an occupier's tongue,

a mouthful to stop
      a mouth, a kiss.
            You pressed

the blade
      of its majesty
            to your lips.

It flowed in you,
      and you in it.
            Flattering fox,

it tried to defeat you.
      You inquired about
            the ransom, didn't you?

9
Did she tell me a dream? Never.
There was a pink Volkswagen to pay for.

Our happiest moment? The Fulford ferry
losing way at night and crashing helplessly into pilings
at Swartz Bay two days before Christmas
with a little fir tree in our trunk.
Sailing home from Marge's.

10

A morning in 1944
      at the Cowichan Bay
            Inn when Great-Aunt

Marjorie—who told
      me over a potato
            one summer day

that rather than
      bear the burden
            of others' misfortunes

she'd blinded
      her second sight—
            assembled her sisters,

her daughter,
      her nieces,
            the cook and

the chambermaids
      in the lounge
            to show them

how to take
      the safety off
            a Lewis Gun

issued to her husband,
        a Vancouver Island
                ranger. If any

filthy Japs
        were spotted
                running across

the oyster beds
        extolled once by
                the *Tatler*

the kitchen bell
        would clang
                and the girls

were to muster.
        There'd be no
                time to lose.

She'd shoot
        each one,
                then the dog,

then herself.
        Anatomical
                details of

tortures inflicted
        by the enemy
                had been lost

on no one. Yet
    on a pretty island
        just up the channel

with their whips
    and straps invaders
        harvesting children

for the Vatican
    would have given
        those Japs a run

for their money,
    in terms of
        technique if not

cruelty. There was
    an eight-foot gap
        between the inn

and the wooden
    home next door,
        and more houses

curving along
    the beach as
        the old village did.

"I don't remember
    anyone living
        there at all,"

said my mother.
      Love in her family
            was in short supply

as it was. Still,
      such a catastrophic
            failure of compassion

and curiosity
      could only
            have been

indulged by
      citizens who'd
            calculated

the benefits
      accruing from
            their neighbours'

extinction.
      The children
            on that island

kept their secrets
      inside
            for years.

At that time,
      you may recall,
            Indians were

not permitted
      above the
            car deck of

the CPR ferries.
      One year
            the girls got

Cowichan sweaters
      from their mother.
            My mum then

recalled an old
      klootch, she said,
            on a fenceline,

picking tufts
      of lamb's wool
           . off the barbs.

11
A vestigial hand left the little slip
      of paper from *Debrett's* with its thin
            italic pedigree on her desk for weeks.

Proof.

"Tell no one," she hissed.

12

With her sisters abandoned to their wounds
she seized high ground
on the island fastness.

"I'm the king of the castle
and you're the dirty rascal."
I believe she taught us that.

13
A day was for disarming
        with gin. No inquests

into inner convulsions, thought or
        sexual rage. Sirens all night now.

A man in a red shirt inside a black gate
        shot down on the street,

police in the house, his wife screaming,
        "My fucking husband's dead ..."

Today you feel everything fraying.

14
somewhere you're

        someone

is tending to you

        rolling you

changing

        everything's

an ordeal

        or lost

how will you

        weather this

waiting

        for your new name?

how will i

        find you then?

15
In an Ottawa spring
      she planted plastic

tulips, their red glans
      rose above the drifts.

All her life she wanted
      to go home.

At shift's end
      the bawdy one

stopped in. Socks off?
      Window open? Good.

We held her tightly
      then let her go.

Now she's away.
      The hawk is in the holly.

16
48°52'001"N
123°33'297"W

17
my father, we are swimming
my mother, we are swimming
in a nation at war

the sycamore's embrace
across centuries
i reach up

grief does not give way

South Slocan

don't
forget
the

wing
tip
the

two
by
four

a
straw
beneath

the
soffit
"clatter

of
conjecture"
manifest

opening
note
of

a
swallow's
nest

A Stick Chart

> [Rimbaud] was pure dynamite, but first I had to fling my own stick.
> HENRY MILLER, *The Time of the Assassins: A Study of Rimbaud*

> *Pouvoir marcher, sans tromper l'oiseau, du coeur de l'arbre*
> *à l'extase du fruit ...*
> RENÉ CHAR, *À la santé du serpent*

antler, apex, arm, arrow, ascender, assegai, axis
bar, barb, barbel, barbule, barrel, bastinado, bat, baton, beam, billy, birch, blade,
      bludgeon, bobbin, bolt, bone, boom, boss, bough, bow, branch, bristle, bud,
      bump, butt
cam, candle, cane, chart, club, column, cosh, crook, cudgel, cue, cuirass, culm, cutlass
dart, descender, dick, digger, dingle, dowel, dowser, drubber, duct
edge, eel
fagot, fife, fillet, fin, finger, flue, flute, foil, funnel
gallows, gibbet, girder, graft, grass, grip
hair, haft, handgrip, handle, helve, hilt, hoe, hose, horn
icicle, isthmus
javelin, jib, joist
kindling, keel, knar, knob, knur, knurl
ladle, lance, lattice, lash, leg, lever, ligature, lintel, lobe, log
mace, map, mast
nail, needle, newel, nib, nightstick, node
oar, omphalos, ossicle
paddle, palm, peg, pen, pencil, penis, perpendicular, pestle, phallus, picket, pike,
      piling, pillar, pin, pipe, pistil, pizzle, plait, plug, point, pointer, pole, poker, post,
      prickle, priest, prod, projection, protuberance, prong, prop, pull, pylon,
que, quill, quirt
rafter, rail, rapier, ray, red, reed, rib, riser, rod, root, rotor, rower

sapling, sabre, scabbard, sceptre, scion, scourge, scull, shaft, shillelagh, shoot, skewer,
    slip, spar, spear, spicule, spigot, spike, spile, spindle, spine, spire, spit, splint,
    spoke, spool, spray, sprig, spring, sprout, spur, staff, stake, stalactite, stalagmite,
    stalk, stamen, stanchion, standard, stave, steeple, steel, stem, stick, stilt, stock,
    stopper, strand, straw, stringer, streak, strip, stripe, strut, stud, stylus, sweep,
    switch, sword, syrinx
taper, thorn, tine, tip, tooth, tower, tree, truncheon, trunk, truss, tube, turret, tusk, twig
upright
vane, vertical
waddy, wand, weir, whip, wick, willow, wire, wishbone
xiphoid, xylem, xylo
yardstick, yarrow
zenith

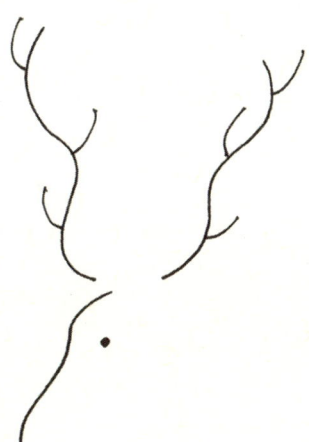

Why We Fight

Nonie

we stood
in the september sun
gazing at the garden stakes
you said,
"you need a garden, don't you?"
i was that bow
with no string

now when i fly over
the pond is choked, the patch of
seaweed-fed kitchen
garden is choked with bristles
of grass
we can't go there now
where once
we were happy

A Capillary Manifesto
November 11, 2010

> *Suppose there is a mast erected, so that one-ninth of its length stands in the ground, twelve feet of it in the water, and five-sixth of its length in the air, or above water; I demand the whole length?*
> DABOLL'S SCHOOLMASTER'S ASSISTANT

One wakes, opens his eyes, the horizon a notch of melon. He reaches for his companion.

One lifts an infant to her hip, takes up her stick and walks out into the sun.

One whacks a blanket. One pokes a lair.

One outruns buddleia water in a field of rye.

What's as bonny, as buttery, or bends like an uncluttered branch?

Who's as true? What pleasure to compare with the peeling of a skookum wand?

What's its equal as defender, driller, handle, hoe?

What's as void of sorrow, shame or rue? As impervious to turning,

or more shapely, tapered by wind, and light?

Many lights make hand work.

Stilt, spindle, wattle, weir.

Cane, stake, switch, spear.

Adam's scratcher, puddle plow, poker, pestle, cockpit rudder. The cock is one, is it not,
　　though its name is whispered?

A twig, but hardly silent.

A punt pole, and for Little John on his log, a staff.

Shaft, stave, strung to a bow.

Incendiary rotor, sycamore scion.

Priest, porter, rib jumper, peg.

An aerial companion, a comfort to dogs.

Stick, I salute you!

Ur-tool, son of rock, thing and thing's progenitor, I celebrate you.

Mud mixer, hoop roller, beloved of boys, how you please me!

Descender, ascender, wedge before bull.

Thing and fetish in one.

Stick, you were my brother.

Xylem inward, phloem outward, phloem inward, xylem outward, honey-green cambium,
　　sapling, sipping, wicking.

One cell plus one plus one.

A manifesto then, from syrinx to syzygy, an invocation:

SINGING, for mumbling

CAPERING, for stumbling

WEEPING, for balking

LISTENING, for talking

LAUGHING, for the face

WINNOWING, for grace

LOVING, for every part

A STICK, for its pungent green heart

unnamed these four-footed
ones dressed as men walking
in the ditch beside me

                their hooves

adepts bending into
what seems
like moonlight

                their horns

in the dark fosse
they're reclaiming
the world

                their muzzles

```
        o   k   a   y   o

        k   a   y   o   k

        a   y   o   k   a

        y   o   k   a   y


o   k   a   y   o   k   a   y   o   k   a   y

k   a   y   o   k   a   y   o   k   a   y   o

a   y   o   k   a   y   o   k   a   y   o   k

y   o   k   a   y   o   k   a   y   o   k   a

o   k   a   y   o   k   a   y   o   k   a   y


        o   k   a   y   o

        k   a   y   o   k

        a   y   o   k   a

        y   o   k   a   y
```

Okay

*Those unwilling to correct their own way of life appear to want
to correct nature itself, instead.*
PELAGIUS (b. Glasgow, 354; d. Palestine, 440?)

Is it, would it, is it, would it,
would it, could it, would it, could it,
might it, might it, might it, might it, might it be, might it, might it,
would it, could it, might it, is it, is it, is it, could it,
if it, is it, would it, is it, is it, can it, would it, can it, would it, be,
okay, okay, okay, okay, okay, okay, okay, okay,
would it, could it, be it, be it, could it be it, would it, would it, would I, could it, if I, if I
I, oh, I, oh, I, oh, I, oh, I, oh, I, oh, I, oh, I, oh,
heigh ho, heigh ho, heigh ho, heigh ho, heigh ho, heigh ho,
ayo, ayo, ayo, ayo, ayo, ayo, ayo, ayo, ayo, ayo,
ayok, ayok, ayok, ayok, ayok, ayok, ayok, ayok, heigh ho, heigh ho,
kayo, kayo, kayo, kayo, kayo, kayo, kayo, kayo, okay, okay,
yokay, yokay, yokay, yokay, yokay, yokay, yokay, yokay,
yoko, yoko, yoko, yoko, yoko, yoko, yoko, yoko, yoko, yoko,
okay, okayo, okay, okayo, okayo, okayo, okayo, okay, okayo,
kayak, okay, kayak, kayak, kayak, okay, kayak, kayak, kayak, kayak,
yoka, yoka, yoka, yoka, yoka, yoka, yoka, yoka, oh heigh, oh heigh,
ayo, ayo, ayoka, ayoka, ayo, ayoka, ayo, ayoka, ayoka, ayoka, ayoka, ayo,
yokay, yokay, yokay, yokay, yokay, yokay, yokay, yokay, yokay, yokay,
koay, koay, koay, koay, koay, koay, koay, koay, koay, koay, koay, koay,
oka, oka, oka, oka, oka, oka, oka, oka, oka, oka, oka, okay, okay,
outa, okay, outa, okay, outa, outa, outa, okay, outa, outa, outa, outa, outa, outa, outa,
yokay, yokay, yokay, yokay, yokay, yokay, yokay, yokay, outa,
ouais, ouais, outa, ouais, ouais, yokay, ouais, okay, ouais, outa, ouais, ouais,
yokay, ouais, yokay, yokay, ouais, ouais, yokay, ouais,
outa, ouais, outa, ouais, outa, ouais, okay, yokay, away, away, yokay, okay, outa,

outa, ouais, outa ouais, the way, the way, the whey, the whey, the way, the way,
the whey, the whey, the whey, the whey, the cheese, the cheese, the whey,
the cheese, the whey, the cheese, the whey, the way they stole, the way,
the way, they way, the whey they stole, the heart they stole, the way they stole
the land they stole, the land away, away, away, they stole, the land they stole, the land
away, the way they stole the heart away, they stole, they stole the heart away,
away, away, the whey, the whey, they gave away, the whey, the whey,
they gave away, the whey, the way, the whey, the way, the whey, the way,
the bay, the bay, is soft today, the land, the land, the bay, the bay they stole away,
the cheese, the cheese, the whey, the cheese, the cheese, the eyes, the ears,
the nose, the knees, the knees, the nose, the nose, the cheese, the knees,
the bay, the knees, the whey, the way, the bay, the way we stole the land away,
the ease, the ease, the eyes, the knees, the ease, the eyes, the eyes, the eyes,
the knees, the ears, the eyes, the ears, the eyes, the knees, down on your knees,
the ears, the ears, oh may I, may I, may I, may I, may I, may I, may I, please,
okay, okay, the ear, the eye, may I, may I, the eye, the eye, the ear, the I,
oh here, oh here, oh please, oh please, the cheese, the cheese, the way, the way,
the whey, the whey, the way, way I, way I, way I, way I, the eye, the eyes,
the ones with eyes, the ones with eyes, the eyes, the eyes, the ones with eyes,
the ones with ears, the ones with eyes, the one with ears, the ones with eyes,
the eyes, the ears, the ayes, the ears, the ayes, the ears, the eyes, the ears, the ayes,
the ears, Algiers, Tangiers, Zaire's frontiers, the sneers, veneers, Mademoiselles from
Armentières, John Deeres, that hat, those ears, that hat, those ears, those eyes, those
ears, those ears, those eyes, those eyes, Shanghai's, Dubai's, okay, okay, what flies, what
flies, wheat flies, time flies, France flies, French flies, France flies, French flies,
France flies, France, perchance, no Morris Dance to jingle the prance, okay, okay, okay,
okay, I may, I may, I may if I may, if I may, I may, I may if I may, if I fall the pole of I
today, okay, okay, if I fall the pole of I today, okay, okay, kayo, okay,
yoko, okay, yoko, kayo, okay, okay, limber, lumber, timber, tumble, timber, tumbrel,
river, rumble, mumble, grumble, Gum-Gum, Senegal gum, spruce gum, bubble gum,
black gum, red gum, blue gum, ghost gum, spirit gum, spotted gum, gumbo, Gumby,

Dublin, Mumbai, Wimbledon, Damson, prune plum, Lamumba plum, plum, plum,
plum, plum, plum bob, plum, plumb, Allegheny plum plum, plum plum, plum,
plum and rum, plum and rum, rum and plum, plum duff, plum pud, pud, pud duff,
ding ding, ding ding, ding duff, ding pud, ding duff, ding ding, plum ding, ding ding,
duff ding, plum ding, plum duff, plum ding, pud ding, pud ding, duff duff, duff ding,
duff duff, duff ding, plum ding, ding ding, plum plum, plum ding, plum ding, plum ding,
pud pud, pud ding, ding ding, plum pud, plum pud, plum plum, ding ding, the plum, a plum,
the holly, the berry, the holly, the berry, the flame, the berry, the tree, the tip, the trips,
the tree, the tips, the trips, the drips, the tips, the trips, the trips the tree tips, the take,
the trips, the take, the tree, the tips, the trips, the drips, the trips the tree tips take,
would it, could it, might it, is it, is it, is it, could it, as it, may it, may I, okay, okay,
yokay, yokay, okay, okay, may I, okay, is it, okay, away, away, away, away, kayak, come
back, kayak, come back, come back, yokay, yokay, the bay, the bay, a way, the way we
stole the bay, away, away, is it okay, the whey, may I, is it, okay, okay, okay, okay, the
way, is it, is it, okay, okay, is it okay, okay, okay, is it, is it, it is, it is is it okay, okay
the eyes, the ears, the nose, the knees, the knees, the knees, the knees,
the tips, the trees, the trips, the drips, the tulip trees, the eyes, the ayes, the ayes have,
the ayes have it, have it, have it, the ayes, the eyes have it, the ayes, the eyes,
okay, okay, is it okay, yokay, yokay, heigh ho, kayo, heigh ho, kayo, okay, okay,
would it, is it, could it, should it, would it, should it, could it, would it, is it, is it,
okay, okay, okay, okay, is it, is it, okay, okay, may I, may I, may I,
may I stay?

```
            a hide              a wing
        growing                    growing
    a wing                             a hide
```

my mother, waking me at four a.m.
"Sweetie?"

at night our names are called
as if they've pulled the cord
to tell us we've reached their stop

our dreams beheaded
for their purposes
what are their purposes?

Meadowlark

George and the big guys rode up one summer day on their old rusty bikes
from Oliver, and after tooling around in the alkali and firing off
a few pellets, he told them he'd sprained his ankle so he could stay
and poke around at the bend to look for fossils.
That's where I found him, a curious boy with a crewcut in a T-shirt
pocketing tiny slabs of ancient seabed stamped with gingko leaves.
I was after shed rattles, and adverbs. After digging
into the bank we went down to the lower field and lay on our backs
gazing up at the sky, with an ear open for snakes,
two guys together, the longer one with a pocketful of fossils.
The bees made noises in the greasewood. Or had he fallen asleep?
"I wonder if we'll know each other when we're old?" I asked.
"Sure," he said, reassuringly.
"Bingo," I said.
"Hmm?"
"Nothing."
We crossed our legs. There were no airliners to mark up the sky in those days, no
telescopes, just crickets and meadowlarks and licks of wind.
"What about babies?"
"What?"
"Do babies know they're babies before they're babies?"
He gave me a look.
"No," he said, then, "Maybe."
He seemed cross.
A young guy can put a lot of pressure on a big guy.
"How the hell should I know," he said.
"What kind of ..."
"What?"
"What kind of food will we eat then?"
"Same," he said after a bit.
"Same?"

"Same," he said, the old magpie.

No one wanted to be a meadowlark.

Maybe one of those babies would.

I was listening to a little bird in the sage. My eyes were shut tight.

George was shuffling through his fossils.

I was watching us way down below lying on the earth

with the ticks and the prickly pears. I was as huge as the sky.

"Hey," he said, "the trick is to forget yourself if you can, even if it's only for a second."

"What?"

He rolled away, and it seemed I didn't know who I was in the first place.

"Gotta go," said the voice beside me. "I shouldn't be here."

We lay there for another second; I held my breath.

"Don't sweat it," he said.

As he got up he punched me on the shoulder.

I could still hear the fossils in his pocket as he took the turn to Fairview.

Then, lying there, I heard a voice.

"What separates you from me?" it asked.

I looked up.

It was a meadowlark, perched on a crown of sage.

It glanced in my direction

and took off.

Bunion Derby

For Jenny Penberthy

> *I'm a leaf among leaves, a caterpillar among caterpillars, and not a differentiated being.*
> JEAN GENET, "Interview with Madeleine Gobeil"

> *I imitated people because I was looking for a way out, and for no other reason.*
> FRANZ KAFKA, "A Report to an Academy"

I'm on
a boulder
in the absent
shadow
of an eroded
mountain
it rolled
down.
Nothing for miles
tops this
saddle
horn.

Pulverized craton
drifts down
wind.
Where are
the martyrs'
boulevards
and crimson
toques?

I'll project celebrant
dents
onto the boulder's
fuselage,
or Éluard's *"Liberté"*
in lichen stains.

Or France. Project France.
France. France. France. France.
France. France. France. France.
France. France. France. France.
Vers luisants / Mirages / mousse au chocolat
France. France. France. France.
France. France. France. France.
France. France. France. France.
Cerfs-volants / daube / Kiggavik / Roussel
France. France. France. France.
France. France. France. France.
France. France. France. France.
Is it not time to wake up again?

      Éluard: "There is another world / but it is in this one."

      Kafka: "We were expelled from Paradise, but it was not destroyed."

One one, one one, one one,
two two, two two, one, two,
one, two, one one, two one,
two two, one, one, two, one,
two, one, one, two, two, two,
one, two, one, two, one, two

two, one, one one, one one
two, one two, one, two one,
one two, one two, two one,
two, two, one, two two, one,
two, one, one two, one two,
one two, two one, one one,
two, one, one two, two, two,
two, one, two, two, one, two,
one.

Their majesties rise & twirl.
We're here to amuse
or (something) them.
She's yanked off her heels.
The emperor slides
down her.

There *are* invisible hours in the day.

In the shadow's chassis
uncrowned poets crow at
the grand old Starlite
smeared with lava.
The prime minister slips
an inner tube into
his trunks.
Then the sun pops up.
The horizon's
Twombly's.

Anemone, anemone,
"*J'écris ton nom.*"

On the twitching mound
a butterflied lung
yields a marine
bottom: hulls
handrails
policemen pierced by steeples.

It's here
among the swan-eating succulents
that they
lock ankles
on slaty afternoons
and mambo
on spilled pearls
clutching each other's
necks.

"Screw the shoes," she thinks.
The dance hall's called
"God is never satisfied."

The nuptial bed's a tomb
if you're lucky.
I've seen them dog-paddling in moonlight
naked as olms
him in his stag head
her with sceptre and mic.

Over the decades
I've grown
women's parts.
I explore them
when you're asleep
by the light of our street lamp
in the falling snow.

At the front, things are deteriorating.
The young: "How do I preserve what I love?"

"Who shall wear the starry crown?"

I'll depend on Onions's
Third Edition,
Revised (1955),
the last entry on
the second last page
in the *Addenda*
and *Corrigenda.*

Staggering against the other, they wave.

waving, waving, wave, waving, wave, wave, sea, see, sea, see, sea, see see, sea, sea wave,
see, sea, waving, see, sea, sea wave, see, wave, see, wave, sea wave, see, wave, wave,
wave, sea wave, see waving, sea wave, waving, see, see, see, see, see, wave, see, waving,
waving, see, sea, waving, see, sea, sea, sea wave, waving, sea waving, wave, see, sea, sea
wave, see, see, sea, waving, wave, sea wave, sea, sea, wave, see, see, waving, waving, sea,
see, see, sea waving sea, sea, see, see, sea, sea, sea, see, see see, see see see, see sea, see

"I'll see you again, whenever spring breaks through again.
Time may lie heavy between, but what has been, is past forgetting.
Your sweet memory, across the years will come to me.
Though my world may go awry, in my heart 'twill ever lie,
just the echo of a sigh,
goodbye."

Valentine

little lamb bone
little shank
who put the penny
in your penny bank?

little sweet lips
little bee
who put the carrot
with the celery?

from Kamchatka

.

typically
I'd be at my post
at that hour
but a jackrabbit

+

the weeks
like letters in a mailbag

+

what Rufus wanted
was a horse
he got a woman

+

in my long life
one sea trout

+

we take to the tub
monthly
like clockwork
except in winter

+

there was a squeak
I rolled it up in my slice of bread
farewell, mouse
you are the fortunate one

+

six children
a grandmother
in less than an hour

+

I've given the best part of my life
away

+

last night
by the moon
the whole bunkhouse
correcting one another's
dreams

+

the entire family
three brothers

+

in her lung
a splinter
Okhotsk again

+

night in its nightie
day in its deity
human animal human

+

one more log
i'll leap the bay
light the candle
if he's away

+

more sinew, brother
if you can spare it

+

my face on me
a string you pull

+

come spring
my head will
grow heavy
with their beauty

Leda

The locomotive that's a city journeys on the
circular track of its origin, its circumference so
severe the engine's bent to its arc and will never be
bent back. Like Rimbaud's abandoned locomotive,
what it is it will always be.

Beneath the rug: a blunder, a birth, a gutting,
an abduction, an occupation, coitus
with a god, a sister & brother hurling
their child into the sea to wash up on the sandbar
where he, with his founder's cross, will bend his knee.

    "But I have a long, inherited neck."

The primal nest is foul with hairballs and sour milk;
the old catastrophe's reprised in this and in every circuit.
When truth is concealed, for shame or
for profit, people are at odds with themselves.

    "Where have we gone wrong?"

When goodness is for sale.

    "How do I look?"

The occupation peaks in a cocked hat. Enter the
sailors, the Seaforths, the honour guard, brass
bands, odd fellows, brownies, firemen, dog packs
and timber-log arches with shaggy legs proclaiming
prosperity. Little kids wiggle flags. Young men await
the scythe. The cinematographer pans his lens at a

solemn 20 f.p.s., then stops. A girl, glowing in her summer
dress, steps onto the street with a box camera. It's
September 18, 1912. The young woman focuses.
A carriage appears. The duke and duchess of Connaught
arrive off-screen. She releases the shutter. They vanish
from the frame and climb the courthouse steps. She
advances the film. She releases the shutter. She advances
the film. She focuses, she releases the shutter. She
advances the film. The camera holds still. The girl
steps forward, takes aim, releases the shutter, advances
the film. The cinematograph waits, like a leopard.

The light hurries to her radiance.
Twombly, I think of you.

What He Knows
For Karl Siegler

Is it a mistake to think anything
you think you think?
                    It is the human mistake.
Is there any deviation in this?
Not in deviating.
Deviating is the human mistake.
Not deviating is the human mistake,
                    really the human mistake.
What can you subtract? Nothing.

To think is to be ashamed. What of those
we think not to mention,
the Acknowledged Legislators,
who rejected poetry to become
war criminals, collaborators, the *unsmashed machines*
with their contempt
                    and their dogs,
and the brilliant weapons men, von Braun,
who was ordered by the U.S. Army to stay away
from the American Academy of Poets
and Robert Oppenheimer?
                    All were paid well,
some in Canadian dollars.

            Who's this?   And this?   Whose face?
            And this one—and she and he and whose
            bewildered face is this?   This one
            and this—and this little face, like a petal
            pressed against the pane?

Benjamin in Marseilles shaking morphine tablets
into Koestler's hands. Some say he was shadowed
by agents of Stalin, another operator
who got too big for poetry,
whose first lyrics
in the seminary in Tiflis
lit up anthologies for a hundred years.

I gazed into the Suffolk sky
Spitfires were puncturing the cloudbanks.
A poet from America arrived
whose name was on the notes.
Imagine a continent as a colander
dedicated to screening out impurities.

The lake above Quilchena where
the prince and princess enjoyed a little
leg-over with the sandflies
planting the flag.

But *larks*! Are they real? Of course
they are. They're not all from long ago.
You can hear them singing beneath
the roar of microphones and the sky.
What if this roar became a supernatural human figure?
It would burn your eyeballs to ashes.
Frankly, this took place long ago.

Eros abandoned adores abstraction.
Poets will always make evil beautiful.
But the flocks of godwit on the River Blyth
will be here when we come back
and we will come back
I promise.

The Busy Rock

*Charlemagne was in this Temple when the angel brought
him the foreskin of Our Lord when He was circumcised;
afterwards King Charles had it taken to Paris.*
SIR JOHN MANDEVILLE
The Travels of Sir John Mandeville

A tower that leans is wondrous, but it's
not the architect of its leaning,
or its wonder. The tower is
an observer of its wonder and its wonder
is nothing compared to the wonder of a kidney.
The durability of a kidney is impressive even though
the best are designed to self-destruct in under a hundred years.
Who decides on these longevities?

The tower you're imagining is a has-been
with a 3.9-degree angle. Suurhusen's tilts
at 5.19 degrees. St. Mauritius is on a slow-motion
face plant into a mile-long landslide travelling
an inch and a half each month. After a quake in 2005
it stood at 5.4 degrees.

What on earth or in heaven is not in peril?

Consider Christ's foreskin. Rubens's Mary
can't bring herself to watch.
Rembrandt's winces in the ranks.
Friedrich Herlin's weir of fingers pins
down the spread-eagled boy.
A bris for a prince on a busy rock.

Seven hundred and ninety-nine years later,
Charlemagne is praying in a dingy
Jerusalem temple when his attention is caught by
a flash of light. He has the impression
the sun has broken through.
The place lights up like an angel.

                               It is an angel.
The one who came to Hafiz?

The next thing he knows the creature is
digging into its trouser pocket.
"I've got something here," it says.
"I think this belongs to you."
Withdrawing a pale hand from
the narrow pocket and gesturing
for the king to extend his palm, the angel
deposits a tiny crisp something like a fingernail
wound into a nest of lint to the left of the lifeline.
It's small and weightless with a slight whiff of spikenard.
Charlemagne sneezes.
"Watch it," says the angel.

The emperor stares at what looks like a hangnail
pulled off a thumb, its shape dramatized
by its shadow. Below his knees,
the sticky mud and straw of pilgrims' boots.
Is he speechless? Is he grateful?
Is the sword burning?
Is that it?

Had someone been saving this little flat bonnet?
If so, who?
Had it been like a homemade rabbit's foot?
Was the mission a spur-of-the-moment thing?
Whose spur?

He gazes at the flake, a small grubby
rind like something you'd take out of your nose;
the angel's gone
leaving behind the vulture prepuce.
Herring are spawning.

What? Is your heart a potato, or a tower,
that you cannot empathize?

What if *this* was the one?

Off it went to Paris, says Mandeville, or to
an alabaster reliquary in Aix-la-Chapelle,
or to Leo III whose subjects
plucked out his tongue and eyes.

In the end, it's a commodity in an ugly box
in a prince's toolkit
devoted to the subjection and misery
of millions. Why did the angel
show up at all?

And how are we to comprehend
this strangely touching incident?

Wonder: the eruption of eternity
into the pudding of the day.

Wonder is the crackling charge between things
that bursts like a rocket on midsummer's night,
lighting up the routes between worlds,
a force that gathers strength
from first breath until it pulls you
across time and continents into the embrace
that is your true destiny—so that it may be said
of wonder: "He brings you to your radiant self."

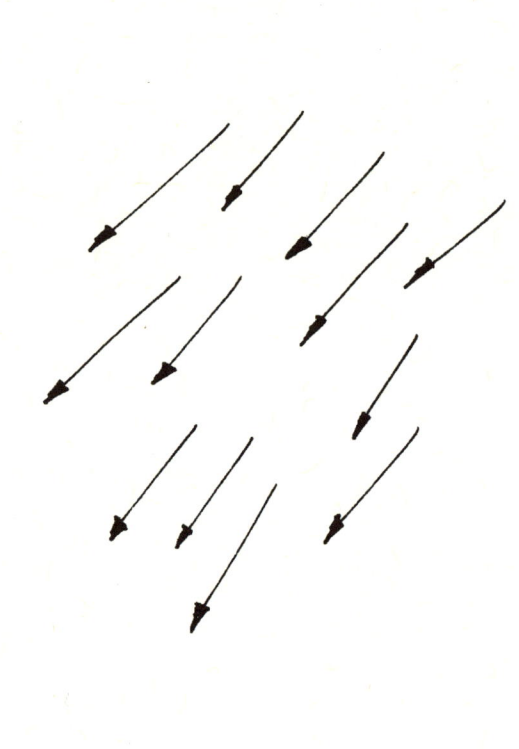

watch out

that pole

is slippery

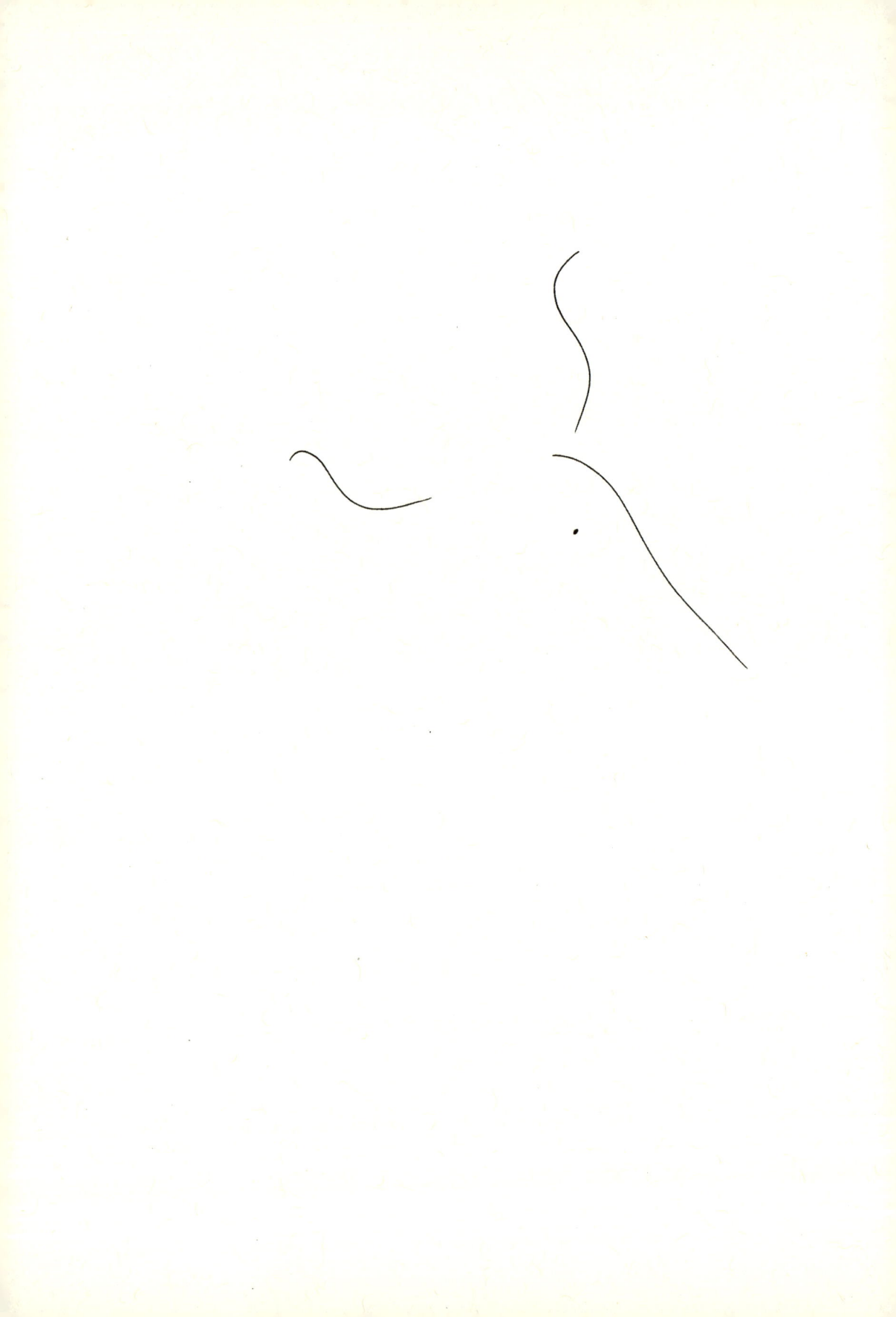

And to conclude, we shall in all things find, that Nature does not onely work Mechanically, but by such excellent and most compendious, as well as stupendious contrivances, that it were impossible for all the reason in the world to find out any contrivance to do the same thing that should have more convenient properties. And can any be so sottish, as to think all those things the productions of chance? Certainly, either their Ratiocination must be extremely depraved, or they did never attentively consider and contemplate the Works of the Al-mighty.

ROBERT HOOKE, "Observ. XXXVII. *Of the Feet of* Flies, *and several other* Insects," *Micrographia: or some Physiological Descriptions of Minute Bodies made by Magnifying Glasses with Observations and Inquiries thereupon*

Sources & Provocations

Agamben, Giorgio. *The Open: Man and Animal*. Translated by Kevin Attell. Stanford: Stanford University Press, 2004.

Alter, Robert. *The Book of Psalms: A Translation with Commentary*. New York: W. W. Norton & Co., 2007.

Anderson, William. *The Face of Glory: Creativity, Consciousness and Civilization*. London: Bloomsbury, 1996.

Auden, W. H. "Concerning the Unpredictable." Introduction to *The Star Thrower* by Loren Eiseley. New York: Houghton Mifflin Harcourt, 2001.

Audubon, John James. *The Birds of America, from Drawings Made in the United States and their Territories*. Vol. 1. New York: J. J. Audubon, 1840.

———. *The Birds of America, from Drawings Made in the United States and their Territories*. Vol. 4. New York: J. J. Audubon, 1842.

Barman, Jean. *Stanley Park's Secret: The Forgotten Families of Whoi Whoi, Kanaka Ranch and Brockton Point*. Madeira Park, BC: Harbour Publishing, 2005.

Barr, Alfred H., Jr., ed. *Fantastic Art Dada Surrealism*. New York: The Museum of Modern Art, 1936.

Barr, James. *A Line in the Sand: The Anglo-French Struggle for the Middle East, 1914–1948*. New York: W. W. Norton & Co., 2011.

Barrett, Michèle. *Casualty Figures: How Five Men Survived the First World War*. London: Verso, 2007.

Barthes, Roland. *What Is Sport?* Translated by Richard Howard. New Haven: Yale University Press, 2007.

———. "Cy Twombly: Works on Paper" and "The Wisdom of Art." In *The Responsibility of Forms: Critical Essays on Music, Art, and Representation*. Translated by Richard Howard. Berkeley: University of California Press, 1985.

Bédouin, Jean-Louis, ed. *André Breton: oeuvres choisies, bibliographie, dessins, portraits, fac-similés*. Poètes d'aujourd'hui 18. Paris: Éditions Pierre Seghers, 1963.

Bell, Julien. "Cy Twombly and Nicholas Poussin: The Odd Couple." *Guardian* (London), July 9, 2011, 16.

Benjamin, Walter. "Letter to Florens Christian Rang." In *Selected Writings Volume 1: 1913–1926*, 387–90. Edited by Marcus Bullock and Michael W. Jennings. Cambridge, MA: The Belknap Press of Harvard University Press, 1996.

———. *Walter Benjamin's Archive: Images, Texts, Signs*. Edited by Ursula Marx, Gudrun Schwarz, Michael Schwarz, and Erdmut Wizisla. Translated by Esther Leslie. London: Verso, 2007.

Berkowitz, Roger, Jeffrey Katz, and Thomas Keenan, ed. *Thinking in Dark Times: Hannah Arendt on Ethics and Politics*. New York: Fordham University Press, 2010.

Biddle, Wayne. *Dark Side of the Moon: Wernher von Braun, the Third Reich, and the Space Race*. New York: W. W. Norton & Co., 2009.

Blaser, Robin. *The Fire: Collected Essays of Robin Blaser*. Edited by Miriam Nichols. Berkeley: University of California Press, 2006.

Blom, Philipp. *The Vertigo Years: Change and Culture in the West, 1900–1914*. Toronto: Emblem, 2009.

Borges, Jorge Luis. *Other Inquisitions, 1937–1952*. Introduction by James E. Irby. Translated by Ruth L. C. Simms. New York: Clarion Books, 1968.

Boulanger, Robert. *Egyptian Painting and the Near East*. Ancient East text by Hatice Nesrin. Translated by Anthony Rhodes. New York: Funk & Wagnalls, 1965.

Breton, André. *Surrealism and Painting*. Introduction by Mark Polizzotti. Translated by Simon Watson Taylor. Boston: MFA Publications, 2002.

———. "Wolfgang Paalen." Preface to the catalogue for the Wolfgang Paalen exhibition, June 21–July 5, 1938, Galerie Renou et Colle, Paris. In *Wolfgang Paalen's DYN: The Complete Reprint*, XVII–XVIII. Edited by Christian Kloyber. New York: Springer-Verlag, 2000.

Bruyère, Bernard. *Rapport sur les Fouilles de Deir el-Médineh* (1928). Cairo: Imprimerie de l'Institut Français d'Archéologie Orientale, 1929.

Bryan, E. H., Jr. "Marshall Islands Stick Chart." *Paradise of the Pacific: Hawaii's Illustrated Monthly Magazine* 50, no. 7 (1938): 12–13.

Burleigh, Michael. *Moral Combat: Good and Evil in World War II*. New York: Harper Collins Publishers, 2011.

Carrouges, Michel. *Kafka versus Kafka*. Translated by Emmett Parker. University, AL: University of Alabama Press, 1968.

Casserley, H. C. *British Locomotive Names of the Twentieth Century*. London: Ian Allan, 1963.

Cendrars, Blaise. *Selected Writings*. Edited by Walter Albert. New York: New Directions, 1966.

———. *Complete Poems*. Introduction by Jay Bochner. Translated by Ron Padgett. Berkeley: University of California Press, 1992.

Césaire, Aimé. *Cahier d'un retour au pays natal*. Paris: Édition présence africaine, 1983. "Au bout du petit matin ..." In his essay "Un grand poète noir," written in New York in 1943 and published as the preface to the 1947 edition of *Cahier d'un retour au pays natal*, Breton wrote: "*La parole d'Aimé Césaire, belle comme l'oxygène naissant.*"

Char, René. *René Char*. Poètes d'aujourd'hui 22. Edited by Pierre Guerre. Paris: Éditions Pierre Seghers, 1961.

Clifford, James. *Routes: Travel and Translation in the Late Twentieth Century*. Cambridge, MA: Harvard University Press, 1997.

Cohen, Morton, ed. *Rudyard Kipling to Rider Haggard: The Record of a Friendship*. Rutherford, NJ: Fairleigh Dickinson University Press, 1965.

Daboll, Nathan. *Daboll's Schoolmaster's Assistant, Improved and Enlarged, Being a Plain Practical System of Arithmetic, Adapted to the United States. With the Addition of the Farmers' and Mechanics' Best Method of Book-Keeping, Designed as a Companion to Daboll's Arithmetic by Samuel Green*. Utica, NY: Gardiner Tracy, 1842.

D'Acres, Lilia, and Donald Luxton. *Lions Gate*. Vancouver: Talonbooks, 1999.

Daphne: A Bucolic Tragedy in One Act. Music composed by Richard Strauss. Libretto by Joseph Gregor. Premiered October 15, 1938, in Dresden. Conductor Karl Böhm.

Davenport, William. "Marshall Islands Cartography." *Expedition* 6, no. 4 (Summer 1964): 10–13.

Derrida, Jacques. *Monolingualism of the Other, or, The Prosthesis of Origin*. Translated by Patrick Mensah. Stanford: Stanford University Press, 1998.

Dickinson, Emily. *New Poems of Emily Dickinson*. Edited by William H. Shurr, Anna Dunlap, and Emily Grey Shurr. Chapel Hill: University of North Carolina Press, 1993.

Duncan, Robert. *Roots and Branches*. New York: Charles Scribner's Sons, 1964.

Edmundson, Mark. *The Death of Sigmund Freud: The Legacy of His Last Days*. New York: Bloomsbury, 2007.
> When Freud's books were burned, the presiding officer declared: "Against the soul-destroying glorification of the instinctual life, for the nobility of the human soul! I consign to the flames the writings of Sigmund Freud." Freud's response: "What progress we are making. In the Middle Ages they would have burned me; nowadays they are content with burning my books" (10.)

Eliot, Valerie, and Hugh Haughton. *The Letters of T. S. Eliot: Volume 1, 1898–1922*. London: Faber & Faber, 2009. First published 1988 by Faber & Faber.

Éluard, Paul. *Ombres et soleil / Shadows and Sun: Selected Writings of 1913–1952*. Translated by Lloyd Alexander and Cicely Buckley. Durham, NH: Oyster River Press, 1995.

Evans, Richard J. *The Coming of the Third Reich*. New York: Penguin Books, 2003.

———. *The Third Reich at War, 1939–1945*. New York: Penguin Books, 2008.

Ferenczi, Sándor, and Karl Abraham, Ernst Simmel, and Ernest Jones. *Psycho-Analysis and the War Neuroses*. Introduction by Sigmund Freud. London: International Psycho-Analytical Press, 1921.

Fienup-Riordan, Ann. *Boundaries and Passages: Rule and Ritual in Yup'ik Eskimo Oral Tradition*. Norman: University of Oklahoma Press, 1994.

Finkielkraut, Alain. *Remembering in Vain: The Klaus Barbie Trial and Crimes Against Humanity*. Introduction by Alice Y. Kaplan. Translated by Roxanne Lapidus with Sima Godfrey. New York: Columbia University Press, 1992.

Fisk, Robert. *The Great War for Civilisation: The Conquest of the Middle East*. London: Harper Perennial, 2006.

Florence, Ronald. *Emissary of the Doomed: Bargaining for Lives in the Holocaust*. New York: Viking, 2010.

Friedländer, Saul. *The Years of Extermination: Nazi Germany and the Jews, 1939–1945*. New York: Harper Perennial, 2008.

"Fugue for Tinhorns." Music and words by Frank Loesser, from *Guys and Dolls* (1950).

Gascoyne, David. *A Short Survey of Surrealism*. Preface by Dawn Ades. Introduction by Michel Remy. London: Enitharmon Press, 2003.

Gallo, Rubén. *Freud in Mexico: Into the Wilds of Psychoanalysis*. Cambridge, MA: MIT Press, 2010.

Gilbert, Martin. *Churchill and the Jews: A Lifelong Friendship*. New York: Henry Holt & Co., 2007.

———. *Churchill: A Life*. London: Heinemann, 1991.

———. *The Holocaust: The Jewish Tragedy*. London: Fontana / Collins, 1987.

Glover, Jonathan. *Humanity: A Moral History of the Twentieth Century*. New Haven, CT: Yale University Press, 2000.

Hafiz. *The Gift: Poems by Hafiz, The Great Sufi Master*. Translated by Daniel Ladinsky. New York: Penguin Compass, 1999.

Halasz, Nicholas. *Captain Dreyfus: The Story of a Mass Hysteria*. New York: Evergreen, 1957.

Harshav, Benjamin. *Marc Chagall and His Times: A Documentary Narrative*. Stanford: Stanford University Press, 2004.

Heinzelman, Kurt, ed. *Make It New: The Rise of Modernism*. Austin: Harry Ransom Humanities Research Center, 2003.

Hooke, Robert. *Micrographia: or some Physiological Descriptions of Minute Bodies made by Magnifying Glasses with Observations and Inquiries thereupon*. London: Printed by Jo. Martyn, and Ja. Allestry, Printers to the Royal Society, and are to be sold at their Shop at the Bell in S. Paul's Churchyard, 1665.

"I'll See You Again." Music and words by Nöel Coward, from *Bitter Sweet* (1929).

Its, Rudolf. *Peter the Great Museum of Anthropology and Ethnography, Leningrad*. Translated by Laura Souders. Leningrad: Aurora Art Publishers, 1989.

Kennedy, Michael. *Richard Strauss*. London: J. M. Dent & Sons, 1988. First published 1970 by J. M. Dent & Sons.

Kennedy, Randy. "American Artist Who Scribbled a Unique Path." *New York Times*, July 6, 2011, A1.

Kimmelman, Michael, *The Accidental Masterpiece: On the Art of Life and Vice Versa*. New York: Penguin Press, 2005.

Klee, Paul. *Handzeichnungen*. Edited by Will Grohmann. Wiesbaden: Insel Verlag, 1953.

Koren, Yehuda, and Eilat Negev. *Lover of Unreason: Assia Wevill, Sylvia Plath's Rival and Ted Hughes's Doomed Love*. New York: Carroll & Graf Publishers, 2007.

Lampert, Tom. *One Life*. Orlando: Harcourt, 2004.

Lévi-Strauss, Claude. *Look, Listen, Read*. Translated by Brian C. J. Singer. New York: Basic Books, 1997.

Lovell, Mary S. *The Churchills: In Love and War*. New York: W. W. Norton & Co., 2011.

Lucian of Samosata. *A True Story*. Translated by A. M. Harmon. Loeb Classical Library no. 14, 247–357, Lucian Vol. 1. New York: G. P. Putnam's Sons, 1913.

Mabille, Pierre. *Mirror of the Marvelous: The Classic Surrealist Work on Myth*. Introduction by André Breton. Translated by Jody Gladding. Illustrated by André Masson. Rochester, VT: Inner Traditions, 1998.

MacCurdy, John T. *War Neuroses*. Preface by W. H. R. Rivers. Cambridge, UK: Cambridge University Press, 1918.

Mandeville, Sir John. *The Travels of Sir John Mandeville*. Translated and with an introduction by C. W. R. D. Moseley. London: Penguin Books, 2005.

Marx, Karl, and Friedrich Engels. *The Communist Manifesto*. Translated by Samuel Moore. Introduction by Martin Malia. New York: Signet Classic, 1998.

Masson, Jeffrey Moussaieff. *The Complete Letters of Sigmund Freud to Wilhelm Fliess, 1887–1904*. Cambridge, MA, and London, England: The Belknap Press of Harvard University Press, 1985.

In a letter to Fliess from Vienna on August 1, 1899, Freud wrote: "Things are incomparably beautiful here; we take walks, long and short, and all of us are very well, except for my occasional symptoms. I am working on the completion of the dream book in a large, quiet, ground-floor room with a view of the mountains. My old and grubby gods, of whom you think so little, take part in the work as paperweights for my manuscripts." Freud is referring here to the small Egyptian, Greek, Mesopotamian and Roman sculptures he kept on his desk while writing, many of them statues of divinities with whom he was, intellectually, in conversation.

Mauriac, François. "Poets of the Resistance." In *Poésie 39–45: an anthology*. Edited and with an introduction by Pierre Seghers. Translated by Roy Campbell. London: Editions Poetry London; Nicholson and Watson, 1947.

Mauzé, Marie. "Totemic Landscapes and Vanishing Cultures: Through the Eyes of Wolfgang Paalen and Kurt Seligmann." *Journal of Surrealism and the Americas* 2:1 (2008): 1–24.

Mekhitarian, Arpeg. *Egyptian Painting*. Translated by Stuart Gilbert. New York: Skira, 1954.

A fresco on the pillar of a Theban tomb from the early phase of the New Kingdom (1530–1520 BCE) shows a male figure, the deceased Tuthmosis III (who ruled from 1504–1450 BCE), drinking from a sycamore tree. With its arm, the sycamore offers its breast to him. ("The King Suckled by the Sycamore Goddess. Burial Chamber of Tuthmosis III, Thebes," 38.) The sycamore is often thought of as the Tree of Life; in Egypt it was associated with Isis/Hathor, the world mother, the goddess of motherhood, birth, joy, music and dancing and love. She brought comfort and eternal life to the dead, nourishing them on their afterlife journey, which is why it's said that the sycamore grows on the threshold between life and death, connecting the two worlds.

Melville, Herman. *The Confidence-Man: His Masquerade*. Edited and with an introduction by Stephen Matterson. London: Penguin Books, 1990.

———. *The Letters of Herman Melville*. Edited by Merrell R. Davis and William H. Gilman. New Haven: Yale University Press, 1960.

———. *John Marr and Other Sailors with Some Sea-Pieces*. In *The Portable Melville*. Edited and with an introduction by Jay Leyda. New York: Viking Press, 1952.

Miller, Henry. *The Time of the Assassins: A Study of Rimbaud*. New York: New Directions, 1946.

"Morgen!" op. 27, no. 4. Music composed by Richard Strauss. Words by John Henry Mackay. Composed in 1894 for Strauss's wife, Pauline.

Moyne, Lord. *Atlantic Circle*. London: Blackie and Son, 1938.

Murray, Mrs. Amelia M. *Letters from the United States, Cuba and Canada*. New York: G. P. Putnam and Company, 1856.

Nash-Marshall, Siobhan. *Joan of Arc: A Spiritual Biography*. New York: Crossroad Publishing Company, 1999.

O'Brien, Conor Cruise. *The Seige: The Saga of Israel and Zionism*. New York: Simon &
Schuster, 1986.

"Oh, It's a Lovely War" (1917). Music and words by J. P. Long and Maurice Scott.

Péret, Benjamin. "The Dishonour of Poets: An Essay on Aragon and Éluard." In *A Menagerie
in Revolt!: Selected Writings*. Introduction by Franklin Rosemont. Afterword by Don
LaCoss. Translated by Cheryl Seaman. Chicago: Black Swan Press, 2009.
Péret's essay is dated "Mexico, February 1945." It concludes: "Every 'poem'
which wilfully exalts an indefinite 'freedom,' even when it's not embellished with
religious or nationalist attributes, ceases first of all to be a poem and ultimately
becomes an obstacle to the total liberation of man, for it deceives by indicating a
'freedom' which merely conceals new chains. On the other hand, from every
authentic poem escapes a breath of complete and stirring freedom (even if this
freedom is not evoked in its political or social aspect), and thus it contributes to
the effective liberation of man" (111–12).

Polizzotti, Mark. *Revolution of the Mind: The Life of André Breton*. New York: Farrar,
Straus and Giroux, 1995. Breton is the French poet in "Herman Melville at the
Morning Star."

Quinn, Ben. "Artist Cy Twombly dies aged 83 in Rome." *Guardian* (London), July 6, 2011: 3.

Rankin, Nicholas. *Churchill's Wizards: The British Genius for Deception 1914–1945*.
London: Faber & Faber, 2008.

Reynolds, David. *In Command of History: Churchill Fighting and Writing the Second World
War*. New York: Random House, 2005.

Reznikoff, Charles. *The Poems of Charles Reznikoff, 1918–1975*. Edited by Seamus Cooney.
Boston: David R. Godine, 2005.

Rilke, Rainer Maria. "Eingang"/"Entrance." In *The Book of Images: Poems*. Revised
bilingual edition. Translated by Edward Snow. New York: North Point Press, 1994.

Rimbaud, Arthur. *Illuminations*. Translated by John Ashbery. New York: W. W. Norton &
Co., 2011.

———. *Complete Works*. Translated by Paul Schmidt. New York: Harper Perennial Modern
Classics, 2008.

Rose, Jacqueline. "Freud in the Tropics." In *On Not Being Able to Sleep: Psychoanalysis
and the Modern World*, 125–48. Princeton: Princeton University Press, 2003.

"Roses of Picardy" (1916). Music by Haydn Wood. Words by Frederick E. Weatherly.

Roussel, Raymond. *New Impressions of Africa / Nouvelles Impressions d'Afrique*.
Translated and with an introduction by Mark Ford. Princeton: Princeton University
Press, 2011.

Sackville-West, Vita. *Saint Joan of Arc*. New York: Doubleday, Doran & Co., 1938.

Seghers, Pierre. "The Conspiracy of the Poets." In *Poésie 39–45: an anthology*. Edited and
with an introduction by Pierre Seghers. Translated by Roy Campbell. London:
Editions Poetry London; Nicholson and Watson, 1947.

Smith, Cyril Stanley. *A Search for Structure: Selected Essays on Science, Art and History*.
Cambridge, MA: MIT Press, 1982.

Spennemann, Dirk H. R. "Traditional and Nineteenth Century Communication Patterns in
the Marshall Islands." *Micronesian Journal of the Humanities and Social Sciences* 4,
no. 1 (June 2005), 25–52.

Stratton-Porter, Gene. *The Harvester*. New York: Grosset & Dunlap, 1916,

Suárez, Thomas. *Early Mapping of the Pacific*. Hong Kong: Periplus Editions, 2004.

The Trial of Jeanne D'Arc.
>Translated into English from the original Latin and French documents by W. P. Barrett. With an essay on the trial of Jeanne D'Arc and dramatis personae, biographical sketches of the trial judges and other persons involved in the maid's career, trial and death by Pierre Champion. Translated from the French by Coley Taylor and Ruth H. Kerr. Illustrations by Frank P. Rennie. New York: Gotham House, 1932.

Twombly, Cy. "Signs." In *Cy Twombly, a Retrospective*. Edited by Kirk Varnedoe. New York: Museum of Modern Art, 1994. First published in *L'Esperienza moderna 2* (August–September 1957).

Ward, Mrs. Humphry. *Towards the Goal*. Introduction by Hon. Theodore Roosevelt. London: John Murray, 1917; and New York: C. Scribner's Sons, 1917.

Warner, Marina. *Joan of Arc: The Image of Female Heroism*. Harmondsworth: Penguin Books, 1983.

Williams, William Carlos. "The Rose." In *Spring and All* (1923). New York: New Directions Facsimile Edition, 2011.

Yeats, William Butler. "Down by the Salley Gardens" ("Gort na Saileán") was first published in *The Wanderings of Oisin and Other Poems* (1889) under the title "An Old Song Re-Sung."
>The poem was an adaptation or "reconstruction" of an old song, probably "The Rambling Boys of Pleasure," that Yeats heard from a woman in Ballisodare, Sligo. It was set to music in 1909 by Herbert Hughes to the traditional air "The Mourne Shore" or "The Maids of the Mourne Shore" ("An Traigh Mughdhorna").

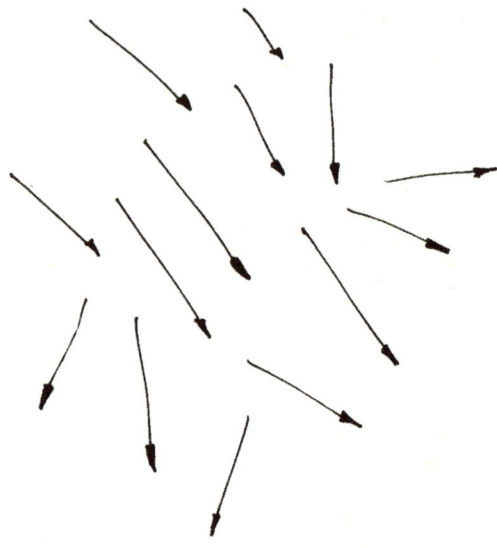

Colin Browne is the author of *Abraham* (Brick Books, 1987); the critically acclaimed collection of poetry *Ground Water* (Talonbooks, 2002), which was nominated for a Governor General's Literary Award and a Dorothy Livesay Poetry Prize; and *The Shovel* (Talonbooks, 2007), shortlisted for the 2008 ReLit Award. He was an editor of *Writing* magazine and co-founder of the Kootenay School of Writing, the Praxis Centre for Screenwriters and the Art of Documentary workshops. Browne's films include *Linton Garner: I Never Said Goodbye* (2003), *Father and Son* (1992) and *White Lake* (1989), which was nominated for a Genie for Best Feature Length Documentary. He is currently working on texts for new operas. His recent work explores the history and legacy of the Surrealist fascination with the art of the Northwest Coast and Alaska, and includes the essay "Scavengers of Paradise." Browne teaches at Simon Fraser University's School for the Contemporary Arts.

o

The cover image is a silhouette of a Marshall Islands stick chart, made by a navigator for himself and his apprentices to help determine their route between islands and beyond. Made from the midribs of palm fronds and shells, its function is to identify wave breaks and swells interrupted and redirected by the many islands in the archipelago. By being aware of interference patterns and swell refraction, a navigator can "see" what is otherwise invisible.

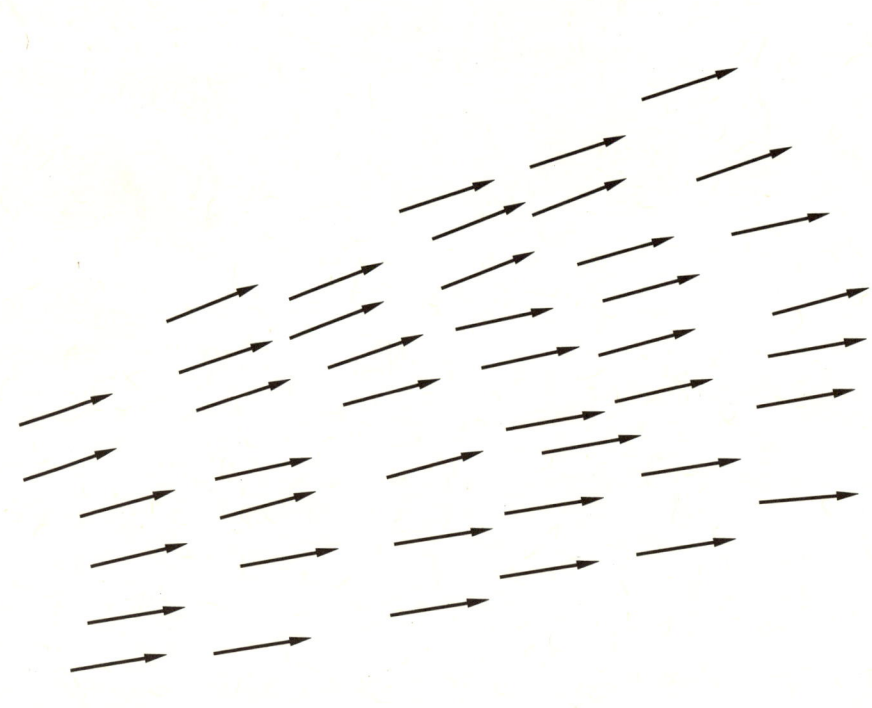